SpringerBriefs in Law

SpringerBriefs in Law and Regulation & Innovation

Series Editor

Kai P. Purnhagen, Chair of Food Law, University of Bayreuth, Kulmbach, Bayern, Germany

SpringerBriefs in Law and Regulation & Innovation present summaries of cutting-edge research and practical applications across the wide spectrum of regulatory law. Regulation has established itself as an important component of the legal system. It aims to achieve the common good in the interaction between administration and private individuals and occurs alongside the other central (administrative) legal functions of limiting state power to protect freedom, averting dangers, regulating the direct provision of state services and the general provision of legal rules for social development. SpringerBriefs in Law and Regulation & Innovation are dedicated to the understanding, systematic recording and dogmatic processing of such regulatory regimes. It is open for basic questions, central elements and new developments in the regulatory law. The focus is on legal regimes to secure results that promote the common good from and through economic competition, such as those found in network economies and increasingly in the food as well as in the health sector etc. Featuring compact volumes of 50 to 125 pages, the series covers a range of content from mainly professional but also academic.

Yen-Lin Agnes Chiu

Money Laundering and Terrorist Financing

European Union Reforms and External Implications

Springer

Yen-Lin Agnes Chiu
School of Law
Fu Jen Catholic University
New Taipei City, Taiwan

ISSN 2192-855X ISSN 2192-8568 (electronic)
SpringerBriefs in Law
ISSN 3004-9210 ISSN 3004-9229 (electronic)
SpringerBriefs in Law and Regulation & Innovation
ISBN 978-981-96-6653-9 ISBN 978-981-96-6654-6 (eBook)
https://doi.org/10.1007/978-981-96-6654-6

This Springer imprint is published by the registered company Springer Nature Singapore Pte Ltd.
The registered company address is: 152 Beach Road, #21-01/04 Gateway East, Singapore 189721, Singapore

Acknowledgments

An original version of this work was first presented on 6 May 2022 at *The EU External Relations under the Global Change Conference* organized by the Institute of European and American Studies (IEAS), Academia Sinica. I would like to extend my sincere thanks to Professor Der-Chin Horng, a Research Fellow of the IEAS, for his kind invitation to attend this conference.

Contents

About the Author

Yen-Lin Agnes Chiu is an Associate Professor at Fu Jen Catholic University, School of Law. Her research interests range from EU law to international and comparative law, with a particular focus on sustainable business and financial law. She obtained a doctoral degree in law from the University of Linz in Austria and a Master of Law (LL.M.) from Columbia University in the United States and is admitted as an attorney in the State of New York. Her academic achievements and contributions to higher education have been recognized with numerous awards. She has also been engaged in the service of public institutions, animal welfare and environmental protection.

Abbreviations

ab initio	From the Beginning
AMLA	Authority for Anti-Money Laundering and Countering the Financing of Terrorism
AML/CFT	Anti-Money Laundering/Countering the Financing of Terrorism
AMLD	Anti-Money Laundering Directive
AMLO	Anti-Money Laundering Office
APG	Asia/Pacific Group on Money Laundering
Art.	Article
BO	Beneficial Owner
CASPs	Crypto-Asset Service Providers
CDD	Customer Due Diligence
de facto	In Fact, In Reality
de lege ferenda	On the Basis of New Law, Future Law
de lege lata	The Law That Is in Force, the Law That Exists, as the Law Is
DNFBPs	Designated Non-Financial Businesses and Professions
EBA	European Banking Authority
ECB	European Central Bank
ECSP	European Crowdfunding Service Providers
e.g.	exempli gratia, For Example
EIOPA	European Insurance and Occupational Pensions Authority
EP	European Parliament
EPPO	European Public Prosecutor's Office
ESAs	European Supervisory Authorities
ESCB	European System of Central Banks
ESFS	European System of Financial Supervision
ESMA	European Securities and Markets Authority
ESRB	European Systemic Risk Board
EU	European Union
EUR	Euro
Eurojust	European Union Agency for Criminal Justice Cooperation
Europol	European Union Agency for Law Enforcement Cooperation

FATF	Financial Action Task Force
FHC	Financial Holding Company
FIs	Financial Institutions
FIU	Financial Intelligence Unit
FSC	Financial Supervisory Commission
i.e.	id est, That Is
in lieu of	Instead of
inter alia	Among Other Things
MiCA	Markets in Crypto-Assets
ML	Money Laundering
MLCA	Money Laundering Control Act
MOEA	Ministry of Economic Affairs
MS	Member States
NCA	National Competent Authority
NDAs	National Designated Authorities
NGOs	Non-Governmental Organizations
No.	Number
NT	New Taiwan Dollar
OLAF	European Anti-Fraud Office
on a par	The Same as, Equal to
PEPs	Politically Exposed Persons
per se	By Itself
potpourri	Mixture
PSP	Payment Service Provider
Rec.	Recital
Reg.	Regulation
SSM	Single Supervisory Mechanism
status quo	Present Situation
TEU	Treaty on European Union
TF	Terrorist Financing
TFEU	Treaty on the Functioning of the European Union
TFR	Transfer of Funds Regulation
ultima ratio	The Last Resort
VAs	Virtual Assets
VASPs	Virtual Asset Service Providers
VCs	Virtual Currencies
VIPs	Very Important Persons

List of Figures

List of Tables

Chapter 1
Introduction

Abstract This chapter provides a brief introduction to the evolution of EU landmark legislation and how the EU has been standing at the forefront of fighting money laundering and terrorist financing, in tandem with the international community. It outlines the legislative history culminating in the 2024 AML/CFT reform package. Against this backdrop, the aim, scope and structure of the book are laid out, along with references to legal definitions of the terms "money laundering" and "terrorist financing".

1.1 Evolution of EU Reforms

More than ever, the world we live in is in need of peace and harmony. Yet, quite to the contrary, antagonistic forces appear to be on the rise. Armed conflicts are proliferating, as militant extremists are fuelled by organized networks often associated with money laundering (ML) and terrorist financing (TF). The escalation of dramatic events has radically altered political, economic and social landscapes, impeding sustainable growth (Ajide and Ojeyinka 2024) on this planet and undermining some of the most fundamental values long cherished by humanity: Security and stability, soundness and integrity, justice and freedom (Bergström 2024; European Commission n.d.) (see Fig. 1.1). To stop these vicious circles of violence, the root causes must be rectified, beginning by disrupting and shutting down illicit monetary flows. With contemporary financial orders inextricably intertwined, this requires that collective action be taken.

Y. L. A. Chiu, *Money Laundering and Terrorist Financing*,
SpringerBriefs in Law and Regulation & Innovation,
https://doi.org/10.1007/978-981-96-6654-6_1

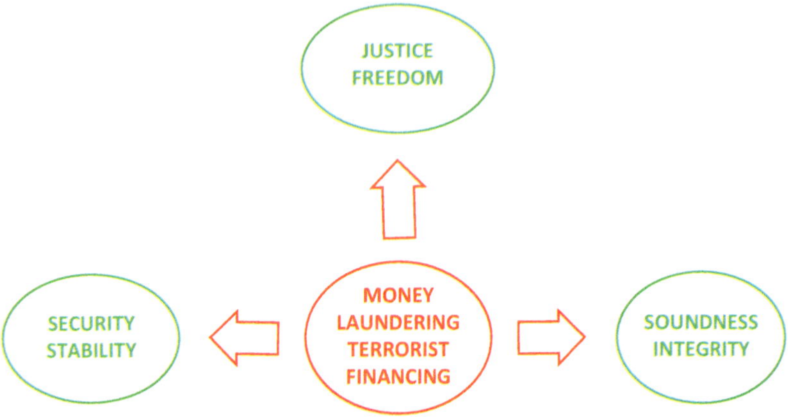

Fig. 1.1 Impact of ML/TF

The European Union (EU) has for more than 35 years been standing at the forefront of fighting ML and TF (European Commission 2020b, 2024). Together with G-7 leaders, the President of the European Commission convened the Financial Action Task Force (FATF) in 1989—the leading standard setting body in this domain (FATF 1991, 2024). At the regional level, the European Commission has been engaged in the Council of Europe, which established a "Committee of Experts on the Evaluation of Anti-Money Laundering Measures and the Financing of Terrorism" (MONEYVAL) in 1997 (Council of Europe 2024) and negotiated the 2005 "Council of Europe Convention on Laundering, Search, Seizure and Confiscation of the Proceeds from Crime and on the Financing of Terrorism" (Warsaw Convention, CETS No. 198) (Council of Europe 2023; European Commission 2005). The European Commission furthermore became an observer of the Egmont Group of Financial Intelligence Units (FIUs) in 2017 (European Commission 2017).

Echoing external trends, the EU announced a series of anti-money laundering directives (AMLDs) in 1991,[1] 2001,[2] 2005,[3] 2015[4] and 2018[5] to prevent abuse of

[1] Council Directive 91/308/EEC of 10 June 1991 on prevention of the use of the financial system for the purpose of money laundering, OJ L 166, 28.6.1991, p. 77–82 (1st AMLD).

[2] Directive 2001/97/EC of the European Parliament and of the Council of 4 December 2001 amending Council Directive 91/308/EEC on prevention of the use of the financial system for the purpose of money laundering, OJ L 344, 28.12.2001, p. 76–82 (2nd AMLD).

[3] Directive 2005/60/EC of the European Parliament and of the Council of 26 October 2005 on the prevention of the use of the financial system for the purpose of money laundering and terrorist financing, OJ L 309, 25.11.2005, p. 15–36 (3rd AMLD).

[4] Directive (EU) 2015/849 of the European Parliament and of the Council of 20 May 2015 on the prevention of the use of the financial system for the purposes of money laundering or terrorist financing, OJ L 141, 5.6.2015, p. 73–117 (4th AMLD).

[5] Directive (EU) 2018/843 of the European Parliament and of the Council of 30 May 2018 amending Directive (EU) 2015/849 on the prevention of the use of the financial system for the purposes of money laundering or terrorist financing, OJ L 156, 19.6.2018, p. 43–74 (5th AMLD).

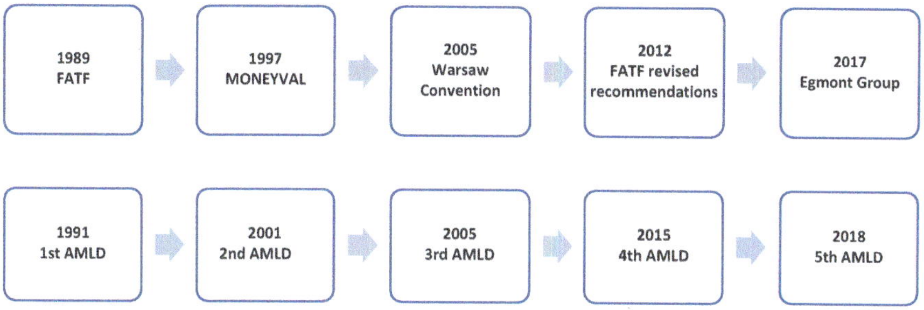

Fig. 1.2 International developments and EU AMLDs

the financial system (see Fig. 1.2). Regrettably, many Member States (MS) failed to correctly transpose the latter two directives in due time, thereupon triggering a wave of infringement proceedings (European Commission 2022, p. 19; Koster 2020). Even worse, high-profile scandals enmeshing European banks underscored how fragmented national laws encouraged forum shopping and made it possible for criminals to exploit unforeseen loopholes (EBA 2022, p. 5; European Commission 2021a).

At the behest of the European Parliament and the Council, the European Commission published an action plan in May 2020 (European Commission 2020a), and on 20 July 2021 tabled an Anti-Money Laundering and Countering the Financing of Terrorism (AML/CFT) reform package composed of four legislative bills (European Commission 2021b). One of the proposed regulations "on information accompanying transfers of funds and certain crypto assets" (TFR)—a recast of Regulation 2015/847—was approved on 31 May 2023 and shall apply starting 30 December 2024.[6] The remaining three proposals underwent months of negotiations until a political agreement was reached on 18 January 2024 and a final compromise text endorsed on 14 February 2024 (Council of the European Union 2024). Treating them as a common legislative priority, the European Parliament adopted these acts at first reading on 24 April 2024 and the Council at third reading on 30 May 2024 (European Parliament Legislative Observatory 2024), just in time before new EU elections were held in June 2024. The regulation "establishing the Authority for Anti-Money Laundering and Countering the Financing of Terrorism" (AMLA Regulation),[7] the regulation "on the prevention of the use of the financial system for the purposes of money laundering or terrorist financing" (AML/CFT Regulation),[8] and an updated Sixth AMLD

[6] Regulation (EU) 2023/1113 of the European Parliament and of the Council of 31 May 2023 on information accompanying transfers of funds and certain crypto-assets and amending Directive (EU) 2015/849, OJ L 150, 9.6.2023, p. 1–39 (TFR), Art. 40.

[7] Regulation (EU) 2024/1620 of the European Parliament and of the Council of 31 May 2024 establishing the Authority for Anti-Money Laundering and Countering the Financing of Terrorism, OJ L, 2024/1620, 19.6.2024, ELI: http://data.europa.eu/eli/reg/2024/1620/oj (AMLA Regulation).

[8] Regulation (EU) 2024/1624 of the European Parliament and of the Council of 31 May 2024 on the prevention of the use of the financial system for the purposes of money laundering or terrorist

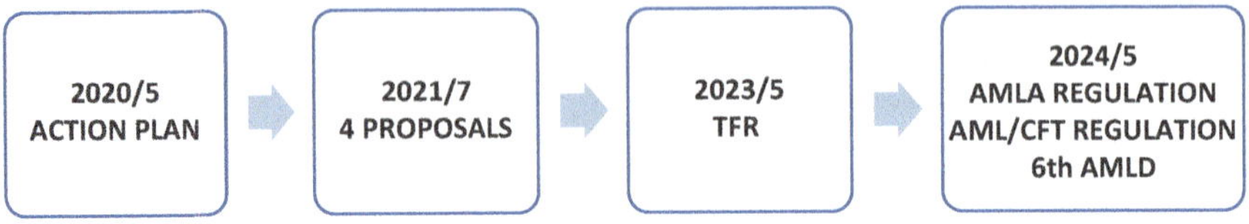

Fig. 1.3 Legislative history

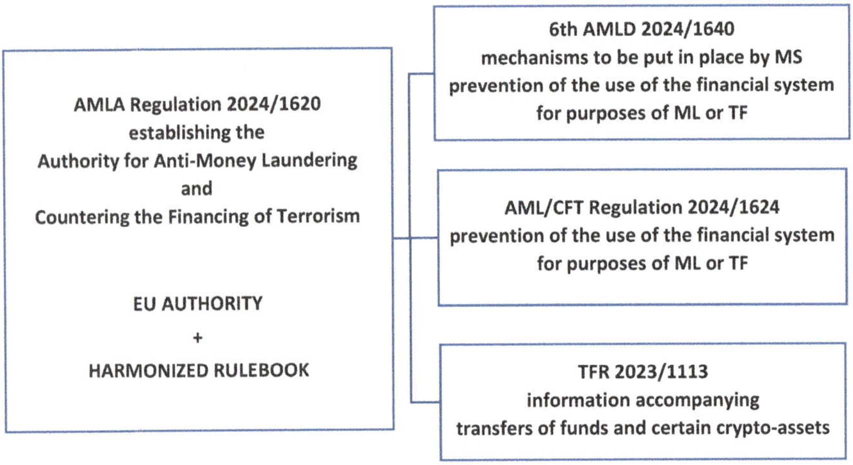

Fig. 1.4 AML/CFT reform package

(6th AMLD)[9] were signed on the first anniversary of the TFR on 31 May 2024, thus successfully completing a legislative procedure that had lasted for three years (see Figs. 1.3 and 1.4).

1.2 Research Aim and Scope

The aim and scope of this book is to discuss the EU AML/CFT reform package with a focus on its outward implications for the wider world. The proposition of analyzing the topic through the prism of external implications is legitimate, as ML and TF must be tackled from a cross-border perspective in order to be repelled effectively, or else

financing, OJ L, 2024/1624, 19.6.2024, ELI: http://data.europa.eu/eli/reg/2024/1624/oj (AML/CFT Regulation).

[9] Directive (EU) 2024/1640 of the European Parliament and of the Council of 31 May 2024 on the mechanisms to be put in place by Member States for the prevention of the use of the financial system for the purposes of money laundering or terrorist financing, amending Directive (EU) 2019/1937, and amending and repealing Directive (EU) 2015/849, OJ L, 2024/1640, 19.6.2024, ELI: http://data.europa.eu/eli/dir/2024/1640/oj (6th AMLD).

the illegal activities will shift to jurisdictions with lower standards. To this end, a combined methodology embedding geographic, historic, teleological, systematic and comparative dimensions is applied in this study. While exploring legal developments within the EU, prospective repercussions are deliberated for foreign stakeholders, such as overseas investors and multinational enterprises, public authorities in third countries, private beneficiaries in distant locations, NGOS, journalists, academics, or tourists visiting the EU. As a result, this work carves out the essence of milestone initiatives enacted in 2024 and presents the findings in a comprehensive yet concise manner.

Before diving into the theme, it is avisable to briefly clarify the terms ML and TF. A lenghty description can be spotted in Art. 1 of the 4th AMLD requiring intentional conduct, both for ML (i.e. conversion or transfer of property; concealment of the true nature of property; acquisition, possession or use of property; or participation in such actions) as well as for TF (i.e. provision or collection of funds), paired with the knowledge that such property is derived from criminal activity or will be used to carry out certain offenses. Following latest reforms, Art. 2 AML/CFT Regulation defines these words quite plainly, by referring to Directive 2018/1673 "on combating money laundering by criminal law"[10] and Directive 2017/541 "on combating terrorism".[11] This emphasizes the coherency between the preventive arm of the AML/CFT framework resorting to administrative law (Schlarb 2022, p. 71) and the corrective arm resorting to EU criminal law.[12] For a comparison of the old and new definitions, see Tables 1.1 and 1.2.

The analysis of the subject matter ensues as follows: Following a brief introduction to the evolution of EU AML/CFT landmark legislation and the scope of this research (Chap. 1), the formal legal instruments are highlighted at the outset (Chap. 2). Given a noteworthy preference for regulations over directives (Sect. 2.1), compliance will be compelling for many affected stakeholders, regardless of their origin or geographic location (Sect. 2.2). In terms of institutional governance (Chap. 3), the construction of a supranational agency with special expertise promises a pioneer leader on the international stage (Sect. 3.1), who will strengthen supervisory convergence within the internal market (Sect. 3.2), while opening up new horizons for global collaboration and information sharing (Sect. 3.3).

The next part illuminates substantive features lying at the heart of EU reforms (Chap. 4), starting with the classification of modern financial intermediaries as

---

[10] Directive (EU) 2018/1673 of the European Parliament and of the Council of 23 October 2018 on combating money laundering by criminal law, OJ L 284, 12.11.2018, p. 22–30.

[11] Directive (EU) 2017/541 of the European Parliament and of the Council of 15 March 2017 on combating terrorism and replacing Council Framework Decision 2002/475/JHA and amending Council Decision 2005/671/JHA, OJ L 88, 31.3.2017, p. 6–21.

[12] AML/CFT Regulation, Rec. 5, noting that Directive 2018/1673 "has led to a common understanding of the money laundering crime and its predicate offences" and Directive 2017/541 "has achieved a common understanding of the crime of terrorist financing. As those concepts are now clarified in Union criminal law, it is no longer necessary for the Union's AML/CFT rules to define money laundering, its predicate offences or terrorist financing. Instead, the Union's AML/CFT framework should be fully coherent with the Union's criminal law framework."

Table 1.1 Definition of ML

<table>
<tr><th>Art. 1
4th AMLD</th><th>Art. 3
Directive 2018/1673 combating ML by criminal law</th><th>Art. 2
AML/CFT Regulation</th></tr>
<tr><td colspan="2">1. following conduct when committed intentionally</td><td>ML means conduct in Art. 3, para. 1 and 5 Directive 2018/1673</td></tr>
<tr><td colspan="2">(a) conversion/transfer of property, knowing property derived from criminal activity
for purpose of concealing/disguising illicit origin, assisting person to evade legal consequences
or participation in such activity</td><td></td></tr>
<tr><td colspan="2">(b) concealment/disguise of true nature, source, location, disposition, movement, rights of property
knowing property derived from criminal activity
or participation in such activity</td><td></td></tr>
<tr><td colspan="2">(c) acquisition/possession/use of property knowing property derived from criminal activity
or participation in such activity</td><td></td></tr>
<tr><td>(d) participation in
attempts to commit, aiding, abetting
facilitate/counsel actions in (a) (b) (c)</td><td>5. conduct in para. 1 (a) (b) punishable when committed by persons who committed/involved in criminal activity</td><td>attempting to commit, aiding, abetting
inciting that conduct</td></tr>
<tr><td>4. ML even where
activities in territory of MS/third country</td><td>3. MS shall ensure that:
(a) conviction for criminal activity not prerequisite
(b) conviction possible without establishing all factual elements
(c) conduct on territory of MS/third country</td><td>whether
activities on territory of MS/third country</td></tr>
<tr><td>knowledge/intent/purpose may be inferred from objective factual circumstances</td><td>2. conduct in para. 1 punishable suspected/ought to have known property derived from criminal activity</td><td>knowledge/intent/purpose may be inferred from objective factual circumstances</td></tr>
</table>

Table 1.2 Definition of TF

<table>
<tr><th>Art. 1
4th AMLD</th><th>Art. 11
Directive 2017/541 combating terrorism</th><th>Art. 2
AML/CFT Regulation</th></tr>
<tr><td colspan="2">provision/collection of funds, by any means, directly or indirectly, with intention that they be used or in knowledge that they are to be used, in full or in part ←</td><td rowspan="2">conduct set out in Art. 11 Directive 2017/541

knowledge/intent/purpose may be inferred from objective factual circumstances

incl. aiding/abetting/inciting/attempting

carried out on territory of MS/third country</td></tr>
<tr><td>to carry out offences within Art. 1 to 4 of Council Framework Decision 2002/475/JHA</td><td>to commit/contribute to offences in Art. 3 to 10 criminal offence when committed intentionally

2. Where TF referred to in para. 1 of this Article concerns offences in Art. 3, 4 and 9

not necessary funds in fact used to commit

nor required that offender knows for which specific offence the funds are to be used</td></tr>
</table>

obliged entities (Sect. 4.1). Their duty to perform customer due diligence must be perceived in the light of dynamic risk factors (Sect. 4.2). Since this includes an understanding of the customer's beneficial ownership, stricter disclosure requirements will make it harder for foreign beneficiaries to hide behind walls of nominees or other legal arrangements (Sect. 4.3). Indeed, any region outside the Union will be screened and encounter tailored measures, if their AML/CFT regime is found to be insufficient (Sect. 4.4).

The last part supplements a case study using the Republic of China (Taiwan) as a concrete example (Chap. 5). A founding member of the Asia/Pacific Group on Money Laundering (APG) since 1997 (APG 2024) and longstanding member of the Egmont Group since 1998 (Egmont Group 2024), this Asian pioneer nation has shown notable resilience on its path of adhering to international AML/CFT standards (Sect. 5.1). As such, it merits a closer look and even serves as a model to demonstrate various degrees of assimilation with western concepts. Comparative outlines pertaining to obliged entities (Sect. 5.2), customer due diligence (Sect. 5.3), beneficial ownership (Sect. 5.4) and sanctions (Sect. 5.5) evidence that Taiwan today has many provisions akin to those of the EU. The conclusion summarizes key insights to help navigate a global financial order that is more inclusive and sustainable (Chap. 6) (see Fig. 1.5).

CHAPTER 1 INTRODUCTION	CHAPTER 2 FORMAL LEGAL INSTRUMENTS	CHAPTER 3 INSTITUTIONAL GOVERNANCE	CHAPTER 4 SUBSTANTIVE REFORMS	CHAPTER 5 CASE STUDY	CHAPTER 6 CONCLUSION
1.1 Evolution of EU Reforms	2.1 Harmonized Rulebook	3.1 EU AML/CFT Authority	4.1 Obliged Entities	5.1 Overview	
1.2 Research Aim and Scope	2.2 Stronger Compliance with Amplified Effects	3.2 Supervisory Convergence	4.2 Customer Due Diligence	5.2 Obliged Entities	
		3.3 Cooperation and Information Sharing	4.3 Beneficial Ownership of Non-EU Citizens	5.3 Customer Due Diligence	
			4.4 Threats Originating from Third Countries	5.4 Beneficial Ownership	
				5.5 Sanctions	

Fig. 1.5 Structure of analysis

Each chapter is complemented by visual graphics and tables to facilitate a better understanding of important terms and key messages. Given the complexity of the legal issues discussed, a didactic approach with carefully designed illustrations makes the topic more easily accessible to readers from various backgrounds. The appendix provides a chronological overview of all relevant laws and regulations mentioned in this book. In summary, this work addresses a global audience and will help readers from around the world realize why and how they could be affected by EU legal reforms.

References

Ajide FM, Ojeyinka TA (2024) Benefit or burden? An exploratory analysis of the impact of anti-money laundering regulations on sustainable development in developing economies. Sustain Dev 32(3):2417–2434. https://doi.org/10.1002/sd.2789

Asia/Pacific Group on Money Laundering (APG) (2024) Chinese Taipei. https://apgml.org/members-and-observers/members/details.aspx?m=28699d47-c110-43cf-883a-e359c2081828. Accessed 2 Dec 2024

Bergström M (2024) The EU's Fight against money laundering and terrorist financing in a digital and fragmented world. In: Bakardjieva Engelbrekt A, Ekman P, Michalski A, Oxelheim L (eds) The borders of the European Union in a conflictual world, pp 177–203. https://doi.org/10.1007/978-3-031-54200-8_8

Council of Europe (2023) MONEYVAL Annual Report 2022. https://rm.coe.int/moneyval-annual-report-2022-web-a4/1680abe10a

Council of Europe (2024) Committee of Experts on the Evaluation of Anti-Money Laundering Measures and the Financing of Terrorism. https://www.coe.int/en/web/moneyval. Accessed 2 Dec 2024

Council of the European Union (2024, February 14) Letter to the Chair of the European Parliament Committee on Economic and Monetary Affairs. https://eur-lex.europa.eu/legal-content/EN/TXT/PDF/?uri=CONSIL:ST_6713_2024_INIT. Accessed 2 Dec 2024

Egmont Group of Financial Intelligence Units (2024) EG Member FIU Information. https://egmontgroup.org/members-by-region/eg-member-fiu-information. Accessed 2 Dec 2024

European Banking Authority (EBA) (2022) Report on competent authorities' approaches to the AML/CFT supervision of banks. https://www.eba.europa.eu/sites/default/documents/files/document_library/Publications/Reports/2022/1028593/Report%20on%20CAs%20approaches%20to%20AML%20CFT%20supervision.pdf

European Commission (n.d.) Anti-money laundering and countering the financing of terrorism at EU level. https://finance.ec.europa.eu/financial-crime/anti-money-laundering-and-countering-financing-terrorism-eu-level_en. Accessed 30 May 2025

European Commission (2005, September 13) Proposal for a Council Decision concerning the signing, on behalf of the European Community, of Council of Europe Convention No. 198 on laundering, search, seizure and confiscation of the proceeds from crime and on the financing of terrorism. https://eur-lex.europa.eu/legal-content/EN/TXT/?uri=CELEX%3A52005PC0426. Accessed 2 Dec 2024

European Commission (2017, July 18) Commission steps up its international engagement to fight money laundering & terrorist financing. https://ec.europa.eu/newsroom/just/items/125759. Accessed 2 Dec 2024

European Commission (2020a, May 7) Communication on an Action Plan for a comprehensive Union policy on preventing money laundering and terrorist financing. https://eur-lex.europa.eu/legal-content/EN/TXT/?uri=PI_COM:C(2020)2800

European Commission (2020b, July 24) Communication on the EU Security Union Strategy. https://eur-lex.europa.eu/legal-content/EN/TXT/?uri=CELEX%3A52020DC0605

European Commission (2021a, July 20) Impact assessment accompanying the anti-money laundering package. https://eur-lex.europa.eu/legal-content/EN/TXT/?uri=CELEX%3A52021SC0190

European Commission (2021b, July 20) Anti-money laundering and countering the financing of terrorism legislative package. https://ec.europa.eu/info/publications/210720-anti-money-laundering-countering-financing-terrorism_en. Accessed 2 Dec 2024

European Commission (2022) 2021 Annual Report on monitoring the application of EU law. https://commission.europa.eu/document/download/793edb79-7b3f-471d-aa9b-679fbcd2e98a_en?filename=com_2022_344_2_en.pdf

European Commission (2024, May 15) Communication on the Seventh Progress Report on the Implementation of the EU Security Union Strategy. https://commission.europa.eu/publications/seventh-progress-report-implementation-eu-security-union-strategy_en

European Parliament Legislative Observatory (2024) Prevention of the use of the financial system for the purposes of money laundering or terrorist financing. https://oeil.secure.europarl.europa.eu/oeil/popups/ficheprocedure.do?reference=2021/0239(COD)&l=en. Anti-Money Laundering Authority (AMLA), https://oeil.secure.europarl.europa.eu/oeil/popups/ficheprocedure.do?reference=2021/0240(COD)&l=en. Prevention of the use of the financial system for the purposes of money laundering or terrorist financing: mechanisms to be put in place by the Member States. https://oeil.secure.europarl.europa.eu/oeil/popups/ficheprocedure.do?reference=2021/0250(COD)&l=en

FATF (1991) Financial Action Task Force Report 1990–1991. https://www.fatf-gafi.org/content/dam/fatf-gafi/annual-reports/1990%201991%20ENG.pdf. Copyright © FATF/OECD. All rights reserved. The official English of the text, as published on the FATF website, is authoritative

FATF (2024) History of the FATF. https://www.fatf-gafi.org/en/the-fatf/history-of-the-fatf.html. Accessed 2 Dec 2024. Copyright © FATF/OECD. All rights reserved. The official English of the text, as published on the FATF website, is authoritative

Koster H (2020) Towards better implementation of the European Union's anti-money laundering and countering the financing of terrorism framework. J Money Laundering Control 23(2):379–386. https://doi.org/10.1108/JMLC-09-2019-0073

Schlarb DD (2022) Rethinking anti-money laundering supervision: the Single Supervisory Mechanism - a model for a European anti-money laundering supervisor? New J Eur Crim Law 13(1):69–90. https://doi.org/10.1177/20322844221085949

Chapter 2
Formal Legal Instruments

Abstract This chapter highlights how the choice of formal legal instruments contributes to the effectiveness of a harmonized rulebook. A noteworthy preference for regulations over directives, along with other components of an upgraded toolkit, promotes legal convergence and predictability, thereby paving the way towards stronger compliance and amplified effects for affected stakeholders, regardless of their origin or geographic location.

2.1 Harmonized Rulebook

The first and foremost change is the choice of formal legal instruments. Drawing lessons from past incidents of delayed or divergent national transpositions, the EU now favors fortified tools in form of EU regulations rather than flexible directives. The underlying motivation is that all Member States should directly apply a coherent and "harmonised rulebook" without protracted national transpositions.[1] Against this backdrop, existing AMLDs shall henceforth be superseded by three EU regulations and an updated 6th AMLD (see Chap. 1, Fig. 1.4).

A shift of power from the national to the supranational level is likewise mirrored in the multitudes of delegated acts, implementing acts, technical standards, guidelines and other specifications EU authorities may enact. Above all, the European Commission is empowered to adopt delegated acts in accordance with Art. 290 TFEU to ensure consistent application and effectiveness of AML/CFT requirements.[2] Technical standards are normally drafted by the Authority for Anti-Money Laundering and Countering the Financing of Terrorism (AMLA) and adopted by the European

[1] AMLA Regulation, Rec. 2, 12.

[2] See AMLA Regulation, Rec. 85, Art. 100 ("Delegated acts"); AML/CFT Regulation, Rec. 167, Art. 85 ("Exercise of the delegation"); 6th AMLD, Art. 71 ("Exercise of the delegation"), specifying the conditions for adopting delegated acts.

Y. L. A. Chiu, *Money Laundering and Terrorist Financing*,
SpringerBriefs in Law and Regulation & Innovation,
https://doi.org/10.1007/978-981-96-6654-6_2

Commission, either by means of delegated acts pursuant to Art. 290 TFEU "to supplement or amend certain non-essential elements"[3] (so called "regulatory technical standards"[4]), or else by means of implementing acts pursuant to Art. 291 TFEU (so called "implementing technical standards") where necessary "to ensure uniform conditions for the implementation".[5] These legislative techniques of devolution are ideal to take into account evolving risks, though it also implies that the battle against ML and TF depends on how details are fleshed out subsequently.

Unlike delegated acts on the one hand, which qualify as a form of "tertiary legislation" the executive is authorized to pass in accordance with conditions laid out in primary and secondary EU law, and implementing acts on the other hand, which constitute a form of executive implementation (Schoo 2019; Gellermann 2018; Vedder 2018), guidelines do not bind the general public. Comparable to recommendations, guidelines are tools to "avoid diverging interpretations of newly adopted EU law" (European Commission 2022), promote "consistent application of Union law"[6] and verify compliance "both proactively and reactively" (European Commission 2023). According to Art. 54 AMLA Regulation, guidelines and recommendations do not have to be adopted by the European Commission but shall be directly issued by AMLA and "addressed to supervisory authorities, supervisors, FIUs and obliged entities." The latter "shall make every effort to comply" or state their reasons for not doing so. The flexibility to either "comply or explain" evidences the non-binding character of guidelines and recommendations. Even so, they may exert some pressure thanks to subsequent publications of compliance reports (see Table 2.1).

Some discretion will still be left to the Member States, where it is not appropriate for European legislators to interfere (e.g. in matters concerning national supervisors or FIUs).[7] In other limited instances (e.g. "to impose additional requirements"[8] or to apply additional countermeasures vis-a-vis third countries) (European Commission 2024a), national preferences will be conditional on the approval of the European Commission. Implementation of planned reforms will be incremental and should be completed by the year 2029 or within three years from the date of adoption (European Commission 2024a). The coming years will thus be a crucial test period for national governments to stay the course and enable smooth operations of the reforms. The outcome, at any rate, will be greater leverage and a much stronger degree of integration, visibly going beyond minimal harmonization (Tiemann 2024).

---

[3] TFEU, Art. 290.

[4] AMLA Regulation, Rec. 12, Art. 49 ("Regulatory technical standards"); AML/CFT Regulation, Rec. 168, Art. 28 ("Regulatory technical standards on the information necessary for the performance of customer due diligence"); 6th AMLD, Rec. 128.

[5] AMLA Regulation, Rec. 13, Art. 53 ("Implementing technical standards"); AML/CFT Regulation, Rec. 170; 6th AMLD, Rec. 130.

[6] AMLA Regulation, Art. 54 ("Guidelines and recommendations").

[7] 6th AMLD, Chapter III ("FIUS"), Chapter IV ("Anti-Money Laundering Supervision").

[8] AML/CFT Regulation, Rec. 26.

Table 2.1 Delegated acts and other instruments

EU MS	PRIMARY EU LAW	**legislative acts** **essential elements** **delegation of power** conditions **confer implementing powers**
EU LEGISLATIVE PALIAMENT COUNCIL	SECONDARY EU LAW	
EU EXECUTIVE COMMISSION	TERTIARY EU LAW DELEGATED ACTS REGULATORY TECHNICAL STANDARDS	**non-legislative acts** general application **supplement/amend** **non-essential elements** of legislative acts Art. 290 TFEU
	IMPLEMENTING ACTS IMPLEMENTING TECHNICAL STANDARDS	**uniform conditions** **for implementing** legislative acts Art. 291 TFEU
AMLA	GUIDELINES RECOMMENDATIONS	addressed to supervisory authorities supervisors, FIUs obliged entities **comply or explain**
	OPINIONS TECHNICAL ADVICE	Parliament, Council Commission

2.2 Stronger Compliance with Amplified Effects

The advantage of increased legal convergence and predictability is that it will create a level playing field and pave the way towards stronger compliance. Stakeholders seeking closer rapport with the internal market or simply visiting the EU (ECB 2022, p. 13) will find it easier to comprehend the rules of the game. For offshore investors and multinational enterprises (European Commission 2024a; Snijder-Kuipers 2023), it could render forum shopping and regulatory arbitrage obsolete, thereby at least partially mitigating (i.e. not completely removing) compliance costs (European Commission 2024b).

These positive effects are reinforced by solidifying the formal status of compliance managers and compliance officers within obliged entities. Responsible for internal consistency and implementation of AML/CFT requirements, they shall be granted the necessary powers (e.g. access to information, direct reporting to management, action to remedy deficiencies), in conjunction with "sufficient human and material resources".[9] Shielded against retaliation, discrimination, unfair treatment or undue influence, compliance officers may be dismissed from office only if the management body and the supervisor are notified. Meanwhile, internal channels must be available for reporting breaches of law, and whistleblowers reporting such breaches shall be legally protected.[10]

As a backup, a palette of remedies can be invoked. Administrative measures range from public statements to discharging managerial personnel, along with cease-and-desist orders or withdrawals of authorizations. Pecuniary sanctions for obliged entities may amount to twice the benefit or EUR 1 million. In the event of credit institutions or financial institutions (FIs), the maximum fine remains EUR 5 million for natural persons, but it has been doubled to EUR 10 million or 10% of the total annual turnover for legal persons.[11] *De lege lata*, members of management and other natural persons responsible for the breach can be punished, and legal persons are moreover liable for persons in leading positions, as well as for lack of supervision or control. Under the new framework, the slate of persons who could be hit with fines has grown appreciably to include trustees and persons holding equivalent positions in similar legal arrangements, beneficial owners (BOs), nominee shareholders and nominee directors.[12] What's more, Member States may ordain higher thresholds and also stipulate private law consequences or criminal sanctions[13] (see Table 2.2).

---

[9] AML/CFT Regulation, Art. 11 ("Compliance functions").

[10] TFR, Art. 32 ("Reporting of breaches"); AML/CFT Regulation, Art. 14 ("Reporting of breaches and protection of reporting persons"), with reference to Directive 2019/1937 on the protection of persons who report breaches of Union law.

[11] 4th AMLD, Art. 59; 6th AMLD, Art. 55 ("Pecuniary sanctions").

[12] AML/CFT Regulation, Rec. 134.

[13] TFR, Chapter VI ("Sanctions and monitoring"); AMLA Regulation, Art. 21–28; AML/CFT Regulation, Rec. 134; 6th AMLD, Chapter IV ("Anti-money laundering supervision"), Section 4 ("Pecuniary sanctions and administrative measures").

Table 2.2 Sanctions

OBLIGED PERSON	
NATURAL PERSON trustees, persons in equivalent positions BOs, nominee shareholders/directors	**LEGAL PERSON** senior management other natural persons responsible for breach liable for person in leading position lack of supervision/control
criminal sanctions	
administrative measures	
periodic pecuniary sanctions	
max. 2 % daily income	max. 3% daily turnover
pecuniary sanctions against credit and FIs	
max. EUR 5 million	max. EUR 10 million / 10% annual turnover
pecuniary sanctions max. 2 x benefit / EUR 1 million	
publication	
whistleblower protection	
private law consequences prohibition to receive profits / exercise voting rights for undisclosed BOs	

The Commision as the executive arm of the EU will be a prominent player in this context (e.g. by formulating criteria for the calculation of penalties) and, in synchrony with AMLA and other specialized authorities, have an upgraded toolkit at hand to guard the internal market.[14] In the face of stiffer oversight and tightly knitted supervision, it will become more difficult to escape sanctions or other substantial ramifications, wherefore it is expedient for anyone venturing into the EU to abide by EU rules, no matter who they are or where they come from.

[14] AML/CFT Regulation, Rec. 135, Art. 68 ("Penalties"); TFR, Art. 53 ("General provisions").

References

European Central Bank (ECB) (2022, February 16) Opinion on a proposal for a directive and a regulation on the prevention of the use of the financial system for the purposes of money laundering or terrorist financing. https://eur-lex.europa.eu/legal-content/EN/TXT/?uri=uriserv%3AOJ.C_.2022.210.01.0015.01.ENG&toc=OJ%3AC%3A2022%3A210%3AFULL

European Commission (2022, October 13) Enforcing EU law for a Europe that delivers. https://commission.europa.eu/document/download/b75864f0-8516-4ff0-9e2a-c3e8a557bbfb_en?filename=com_2022_518_1_en.pdf

European Commission (2023, July) Better Regulations Toolbox. https://commission.europa.eu/document/download/9c8d2189-8abd-4f29-84e9-abc843cc68e0_en?filename=BR%20toolbox%20-%20Jul%202023%20-%20FINAL.pdf

European Commission (2024a, April 24) Questions and Answers: Anti-Money Laundering and Countering Financing of Terrorism (AML/CFT). https://finance.ec.europa.eu/document/download/553ff649-fce8-4e31-b54c-01f562ca0bb3_en?filename=240424-anti-money-laundering-faqs_en.pdf

European Commission (2024b, April 24) Factsheet: Stronger EU rules to fight financial crime. https://finance.ec.europa.eu/financial-crime/amla/stronger-eu-rules-fight-financial-crime_en

Gellermann M (2018) Art. 290 AEUV. In: Streinz R (ed) EUV / AEUV, 3rd edn. C.H. BECK, pp 2393–2396

Schoo J (2019) Artikel 291 AEUV. In: Schwarze J, Becker U, Hatje A, Schoo J (eds) EU-Kommentar, 4th edn. Nomos, pp 3042–3046

Snijder-Kuipers B (2023) Navigating the anti-money laundering landscape – the role companies play in protecting the financial system. IBFD - Fin Capital Markets 24(4). https://www.ibfd.org/sites/default/files/2024-01/selected-journal-articles-ibfd-fcm-aml-2.pdf

Tiemann M (2024) A commentary on the EU money laundering reform in light of the subsidiarity principle. J Fin Regul Compliance 32(3):372–378. https://doi.org/10.1108/JFRC-10-2023-0172

Vedder C (2018) Artikel 290 AEUV. In: Vedder C, Heintschel von Heinegg W (eds) Europäisches Unionsrecht, 2nd edn. Nomos, pp 1167–1172

Chapter 3
Institutional Governance

Abstract This chapter explicates the restructuring of institutional governance. The creation of a new supranational authority with expert skills and concentrated powers promises a pioneer leader on the international stage, who will strengthen supervisory convergence within the internal market, while opening up new horizons for global collaboration and information sharing. A comparison with the European System of Financial Supervision (ESFS) and the Single Supervisory Mechanism (SSM) reveals how the integrated AML/CFT supervisory system distinguishes itself through a broad horizon that is neither confined to the financial sector nor to European boundaries.

3.1 EU AML/CFT Authority

The most tangible symbol of recent reforms is the launch of a specialized[1] "Union body with legal personality" called the "Authority for Anti-Money Laundering and Countering the Financing of Terrorism" (AMLA).[2] Seated in Frankfurt am Main, Germany,[3] AMLA is located in the same city as the European Central Bank (ECB), the European Systemic Risk Board (ESRB) and the European Insurance and Occupational Pensions Authority (EIOPA), with the European Banking Authority (EBA) and the European Securities and Markets Authority (ESMA) not far away in the French capital of Paris. Joining the ranks of these supranational watchdogs, AMLA's mandate is "to protect the public interest, the stability … of the Union's financial system, and the proper functioning of the internal market".[4] Very remarkably, AMLA is taking over AML/CFT related tasks that have so far been assigned to the EBA (EBA n.d., 2020; EU 2024; Pavlidis 2024),[5] while clearly distinguishing itself through a

[1] AMLA Regulation, Rec. 8, 10.

[2] AMLA Regulation, Art. 1 ("Establishment and scope of action"), Art. 3 ("Legal status").

[3] AMLA Regulation, Art. 4 ("Seat").

[4] AMLA Regulation, Art. 1(3).

[5] AMLA Regulation, Rec. 84, Art. 5 ("Tasks"), Art. 103 ("Amendments to Regulation (EU) No. 1093/2010").

Y. L. A. Chiu, *Money Laundering and Terrorist Financing*,
SpringerBriefs in Law and Regulation & Innovation,
https://doi.org/10.1007/978-981-96-6654-6_3

Table 3.1 Mission and objectives

	EBA	ESMA	EIOPA	ESRB	ECB	AMLA
ESTABLISHED	2011				1998/2013	2024
SEAT	Paris, France		Frankfurt am Main, Germany			
LEGAL STATUS	Union body legal personality				EU institution legal personality	Union body legal personality
INDEPENDENCE	shall act/perform their duties independently/impartially/objectively, in the interest of the Union as a whole					
MISSION AND OBJECTIVES	supervisory convergence					
	financial stability in Union, functioning/ integrity of internal market					
	prevent the use of financial system for ML/TF purposes					*prevent the use of financial system for ML/TF purposes*
	credit/other risks	investment/other risks	risks related to (re)insurance, occupational pensions	systemic/macroprudential risks	risks for safety/soundness of credit institutions	ML/TF risks outside Union impact internal market
LEGAL BASIS	Reg. 1093/2010	Reg. 1095/2010	Reg. 1094/2010	Reg. 1092/2010	Reg. 1024/2013 Reg. 468/2014 Art. 13 TEU Art. 282-284 TFEU	Reg. 2024/1620

broad horizon that is neither confined to the financial sector nor to European boundaries: Entrepreneurs operating in third countries, including non-financial obliged entities, and their competent supervisors, for instance, all fall within its ambit (see Table 3.1).

Legally established on 26 June 2024 and initally operated by the European Commission, AMLA is scheduled to assume most of its operations by July 2025, take over the management of FIU.net by July 2027 and commence direct supervision of obliged entities in 2028 (AMLA 2024).[6] It will lend its expertise to the European Commission and be involved in the latter's EU wide risk assessment.[7] Compared with the Commission's inward concentration on ML/TF risks "affecting the internal market and relating to cross-border activities",[8] AMLA has a pronounced external orientiation: It will systematically "monitor developments in third countries and assess … their AML/CFT systems",[9] identify "risks and threats originating from outside the Union" that could potentially impact the internal market,[10] and adopt guidelines on "risks, trends and methods involving any geographical area outside the Union to which obliged entities are exposed."[11]

---

[6] AMLA Regulation, Rec. 86, Art. 107 ("Commencement of the Authority's activities"); 6th AMLD, Art. 73 ("Transitional management of FIU.net").

[7] 6th AMLD, Art. 7(6).

[8] 6th AMLD, Art. 7(1).

[9] AMLA Regulation, Art. 5(1)(b).

[10] AMLA Regulation, Art. 1(3)(b).

[11] AML/CFT Regulation, Art. 32 ("Guidelines on money laundering and terrorist financing risks, trends and methods").

Correlating with such expansive tasks, AMLA possesses abundant powers[12] and has at its disposal a whole spectrum of tools,[13] such as drafting technical standards,[14] issuing guidelines and recommendations,[15] providing opinions and technical advice,[16] making binding decisions,[17] making requests for information,[18] conducting investigations[19] and on-site inspections,[20] applying administrative measures,[21] imposing pecuniary sanctions,[22] carrying out mediation[23] and settling disagreements in cross-border situations[24] (see Table 3.2).

When performing their duties, AMLA's Chair, members of the General Board, the five full-time members of the Executive Board, the Executive Director, and the five members of the Administrative Board of Review "shall act independently and objectively in the interest of the Union as a whole".[25] One might wonder whether so much freedom is matched by adequate accountability, as has been criticized in the aftermath of conferring supervisory powers on the ECB (Kern 2016, p. 482). A comparison with the institutional independence guaranteed under the European System of Financial Supervision (ESFS) and the Single Supervisory Mechanism

---

[12] AMLA Regulation, Art. 6 ("Powers of the Authority").

[13] AMLA Regulation, Section 7 ("Common Instruments").

[14] AMLA Regulation, Art. 49 ("Regulatory technical standards"), Art. 53 ("Implementing technical standards").

[15] AMLA Regulation, Art. 54 ("Guidelines and recommendations"); AML/CFT Regulation, Rec. 31 (content of business-wide risk assessment), Rec. 50 (outsourcing), Rec. 72 (monitoring of business relationships and transactions), Rec. 90 (level of risks associated with PEPs), Rec. 96 (close associates), Rec. 103 (third-party reliance), Art. 9 (internal policies, procedures and controls), Art. 10 (business-wide risk assessment), Art. 18 (outsourcing), Art. 20 (risk factors to be taken into account by obliged entities when entering into business relationships or carrying out occasional transactions), Art. 21 (measures by credit institutions and FIs to ensure compliance with AML/CFT rules), Art. 26 (ongoing monitoring of business relationship), Art. 32 (risks, trends and methods involving geographical areas outside the Union), Art. 34 (customer holding assets of EUR 50 million), Art. 37 (cross-border correspondent relationships for crypto-asset service providers), Art. 40 (transactions with self-hosted address), Art. 42 (PEPs), Art. 50 (reliance on other obliged entities), Art. 69 (suspicious activity or behaviours).

[16] AMLA Regulation, Art. 55 ("Opinions and technical advice").

[17] AMLA Regulation, Art. 6 ("Powers of the Authority").

[18] AMLA Regulation, Art. 17 ("Requests for information").

[19] AMLA Regulation, Art. 18 ("General investigations").

[20] AMLA Regulation, Art. 19 ("On-site inspections").

[21] AMLA Regulation, Art. 21 ("Administrative measures").

[22] AMLA Regulation, Art. 22 ("Pecuniary sanctions"), Art. 23 ("Periodic penalty payments").

[23] AMLA Regulation, Art. 46 ("Mediation between FIUs").

[24] AMLA Regulation, Art. 33 ("Settlement of disagreements between financial supervisors in cross-border situations"), Art. 38 ("Settlement of disagreements between non-financial supervisors in cross-border situations").

[25] AMLA Regulation, Rec. 6, 63, 66, 67, Art. 59 ("Independence of the General Board"), Art. 63 ("Composition and appointment of the Executive Board"), Art. 68 ("Appointment of the Chair of the Authority"), Art. 70 ("Appointment of the Executive Director"), Art. 73 ("Members of the Administrative Board of Review").

Table 3.2 Tasks and powers of AMLA

TASKS (Art. 5)	**POWERS (Art. 6)**
ML/TF RISKS FACING INTERNAL MARKET monitor, assess establish central AML/CFT database share information, train	draft regulatory/implementing technical standards (Art. 49, 53) issue guidelines and recommendations (Art. 54) opinions to Parliament, Council, Commission (Art. 55)
SELECTED OBLIGED ENTITIES compliance group-wide supervision	supervisory/investigative powers (Art. 17-21) pecuniary sanctions, periodic penalty payments (Art. 22-23) instruct/exercise powers of financial supervisors binding decisions, administrative measures
FINANCIAL/NON-FINANCIAL SUPERVISORS convergence of supervisory practices AML/CFT supervisory colleges assessments, peer review assist, mediate	require information/documents/explanations guidelines, recommendations requests to act, instruct on measures to be taken mediate, settle disagreements
FIUS in MS support, coordinate, joint analyses peer review, train, mediate host FIU.net	guidelines, recommendations collect/process information request data/analyses

(SSM) is reassuring: Not only is AMLA directly accountable to the European Parliament (EP) and the Council, as well as obligated to submit annual reports to the Commission.[26] Surpassing accountability requirements of the EBA and even more so of the ECB, AMLA must also provide the European Parliament with comprehensive meeting records comprising an annotated list of decisions each time the General Board convenes.[27] Apart from that, the Chair may be requested to make a statement before relevant committees of the European Parliament, to answer any questions, and to hold confidential discussions behind closed doors.[28] Last but not least, the confidentiality clause in matters concerning AMLA's contributions in international fora is formulated in a less ambiguous and more straightforward manner (see Table 3.3).

[26] AMLA Regulation, Rec. 72.

[27] AMLA Regulation, Art. 84(4).

[28] AMLA Regulation, Art. 84(3), 84(6).

Table 3.3 Accountability

	AMLA	EBA	ECB
ACCOUNTABLE TO	EP, Council		
ANNUAL REPORT TO	EP, Council, Commission		
	include relevant information requested by EP on an ad hoc basis		
PUBLIC PRESENTATION	Chair of AMLA		Chair of ECB Supervisory Board
HEARING	at request of EP		
	shall take place at least annually		
CHAIRPERSON STATEMENT, Q&A	EP committees at request of EP	EP whenever requested	
MEETING RECRODS	within 6 weeks AMLA shall provide EP with comprehensive record of proceedings incl. list of decisions		
RESPONSE TO EP	orally or in writing, within 5 weeks of receipt		orally or in writing
CONFIDENTIAL ORAL DISCUSSIONS	competent EP committees	Chair, Vice-Chairs, Coordinators of competent EP committee	Chair, Vice-Chairs of competent EP committee
CONFIDENTIALITY INTERNATIONAL FORA	When informing EP pertaining to the Authorities' contribution in international fora, the Authority shall not disclose any info it received in performance of that task where such info is subject to confidentiality requirements imposed by third parties.	**Without prejudice to confidentiality obligations** stemming from participation in international fora, the Authority shall inform EP upon request about its contribution to united/common/consistent/effective representation of Union's interests in international fora.	
LEGAL BASIS	Art. 84 Reg. 2024/1620	Art. 3 Reg. 1093/2010	Art. 20 Reg. 1024/2013

3.2 Supervisory Convergence

The blueprint for the AML/CFT architecture was inspired by the Single Supervisory Mechanism (SSM) conceived a decade ago in the aftermath of the global financial crisis (Schlarb 2022, p. 3). To break vicious circles between troubled banks and sovereign debt, Basic SSM Regulation No. 1024/2013[29] and SSM Framework Regulation No. 468/2014[30] conferred on the ECB the prudential supervision of credit institutions in participating Member States, with national competent authorities (NCAs) assuming assisting and implementing roles. Not only did stringent supervision at an elevated level reduce regional partisanship and spur the effective transmission of aspired policies, it also generated positive synergies in terms of available resources, skills and knowledge (Maddaloni and Scopelliti 2022, pp. 34–48). Concurrently, the benefits of local self-governance (e.g. better access to information thanks to geographic proximity) were preserved, wherefore this kind of compromise between centralized and decentralized supervision has been described as overall satisfactory (Maddaloni and Scopelliti 2022).

Continuing a trajectory of supervisory convergence[31] that has been transforming the EU financial system in general and the banking sector in particular, AMLA builds on genuine experiences of the ECB (Kern 2016, pp. 477, 480), EBA, ESMA, EIOPA, and the ESRB. Yet, it leaves behind narrowly defined tasks and embarks on a voyage that merges both micro- and macro-prudential oversight over FIs as well as non-financial entities. The outcome is an integrated (European Commission 2024b) AML/CFT supervisory system[32] that encapsulates the strengths of the European System of Financial Supervision (ESFS) and of the Single Supervisory Mechanism (SSM), without surrendering the principles of autonomous decisionmaking and decentralization (Van den Broek 2014) (see Table 3.4).

Envisaging a supervisory methodology that is both harmonized and objective,[33] AMLA will be guided by a "risk-based approach"[34] using predefined parameters

[29] Council Regulation (EU) No. 1024/2013 of 15 October 2013 conferring specific tasks on the European Central Bank concerning policies relating to the prudential supervision of credit institutions, OJ L 287, 29.10.2013, p. 63–89 (Basic SSM Regulation).

[30] Regulation (EU) No. 468/2014 of the European Central Bank of 16 April 2014 establishing the framework for cooperation within the Single Supervisory Mechanism between the European Central Bank and national competent authorities and with national designated authorities, OJ L 141, 14.5.2014, p. 1–50 (SSM Framework Regulation).

[31] AMLA Regulation, Rec. 9–11, 33, 39, Art. 1(3)(d), Art. 5(3)(e), Art. 5(4)(e), Art. 30 ("Assessments of the state of supervisory convergence"), Art. 35 ("Peer reviews").

[32] According to AMLA Regulation, Art. 2(1)(3) the term "AML/CFT supervisory system" refers to AMLA and "the supervisory authorities in the Member States".

[33] AMLA Regulation, Rec. 2, 10, 12, 16, 21–23, 33, 55, Art. 8 ("AML/CFT supervisory methodology"), Art. 35 ("Peer reviews").

[34] AMLA Regulation, Rec. 10, Art. 8 ("AML/CFT supervisory methodology"). Previously, the 4th AMLD, Art. 48(10) as amended by Directive 2019/2177 mandated the EBA to issue guidelines for risk-based supervision.

Table 3.4 Comparison between ESFS, SSM and AML/CFT supervisory system

European System of Financial Supervision (ESFS)		**Single Supervisory Mechanism (SSM)**		**AML/CFT supervisory system**
ESRB	**ESAs**	**ECB**		**AMLA**
macro-prudential oversight EU financial system	micro-prudential oversight financial institutions	prudential supervision (significant) credit institutions, (mixed) FHCs parent established in participating MS		AML/CFT supervision (selected) obliged entities **including non-financial entities**
in cooperation with competent/supervisory/designated authorities in (participating) MS				
Reg. 1092/2010	Reg. 1093/2010 Reg. 1094/2010 Reg. 1095/2010	Basic SSM Reg. 1024/2013	SSM Framework Reg. 468/2014	Reg. 2024/1620

that include *inter alia* customers, products, services, transactions and delivery channels, as well as geographic areas (e.g. proportion of non-resident customers from designated third countries, correspondent banking services provided in designated third countries, volume of anonymous products, services or transactions).[35] The same standards shall apply even where obliged entities are part of a group that has establishments outside the EU, in which case the competent authorities where the parent undertaking is established shall be responsible for ensuring group-wide compliance.[36]

Where the law of a third country does not permit the implementation of EU AML/CFT requirements (e.g. insufficient level of data protection), the parent undertaking shall take "additional measures" and inform the supervisors of its home MS, who may take a range of actions (e.g. prohibit entering into a business relationship, terminate existing ones, refrain from transactions, shut down third country operations).[37] By all means, supervisors (including AMLA) shall inform each other and pursue a coordinated solution.[38] In all foregoing scenarios, AMLA shall draft and the European Commission is empowered to adopt technical standards,[39] for instance specifying minimum requirements for group-wide policies, extending respective obligations to similar structures (e.g. networks or partnerships that are characterized by common ownership, management or compliance control),[40] or setting forth additional measures and supervisory actions to be taken in countries with lower requirements.[41]

The oversight of obliged entities under the leadership of AMLA[42] can be carried out directly via joint supervisory teams[43] (notably with regard to selected obliged

---

35 AMLA Regulation, Art. 8 ("AML/CFT supervisory methodology"), Art. 12(5).

36 AML/CFT Regulation, Rec. 43, Art. 16 ("Group-wide requirements") calls on the parent undertaking to ensure group-wide compliance. The same principle was previously enshrined in the 4th AMLD, Art. 45(1) requiring obliged entities to apply "group-wide policies". According to the 4th AMLD as amended by the 5th AMLD, Art. 48(5) the effective implementation of group-wide policies and procedures shall be supervised by the competent authorities of the Member State where a parent undertaking is established.

37 AML/CFT Regulation, Rec. 46, Art. 17 (" Branches and subsidiaries in third countries").

38 6th AMLD, Rec. 98–99, Art. 48 ("Exchange of information in relation to implementation of group-wide policies in third countries"). Previously, the 4th AMLD, Art. 45(4) as amended by Directive 2019/2177 provided that MS and EBA shall inform each other.

39 *De lege lata*, additional measures are prescribed by Commission Delegated Regulation (EU) 2019/758 of 31 January 2019 supplementing Directive (EU) 2015/849 of the European Parliament and of the Council with regard to regulatory technical standards for the minimum action and the type of additional measures credit and financial institutions must take to mitigate money laundering and terrorist financing risk in certain third countries, OJ L 125, 14.5.2019, p. 4–10.

40 AML/CFT Regulation, Rec. 168, Art. 16(4).

41 AML/CFT Regulation, Rec. 46, Art. 17(3). Previously, the authority to draft regulatory technical standards belonged to the EBA; see 4th AMLD, Art. 45(6) as amended by Directive 2019/2177.

42 AMLA Regulation, Art. 5(2)(c).

43 AMLA Regulation, Rec. 26.

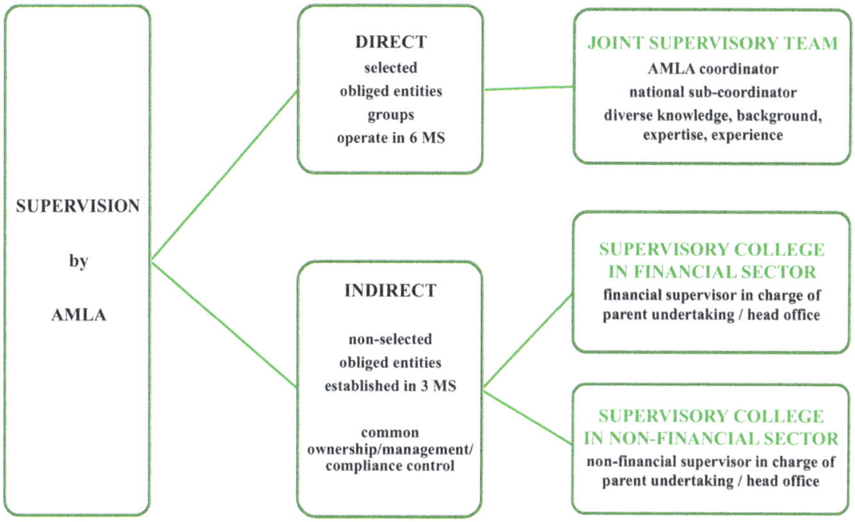

Fig. 3.1 Difference between joint supervisory team and supervisory college

entities that operate in at least six MS, including multinational groups[44] that have headquarters, subsidiaries or branches outside the Union),[45] or indirectly via supervisory colleges (e.g. where non-selected obliged entities or third country entities have set up establishments in three MS)[46] (see Figs. 3.1 and 3.2).

Interestingly enough, the new AML/CFT framework term does not specify the term "joint supervisory team", probably because it is already defined in Art. 2(6) SSM Framework Regulation No. 468/2014 as "a team of supervisors in charge of the supervision of a significant supervised entity or a significant supervised group". The new provisions do, however, stress that joint supervisory teams be "composed of staff with a sufficient level of knowledge, expertise and experience, and with sufficiently diverse knowledge, backgrounds, expertise and experience", thereby attaching particular importance to the qualification and diversity of team members (see Table 3.5).

---

[44] A group is defined in the 4th AMLD, Art. 3(15) and AML/CFT Regulation, Art. 2(1)(41) with reference to Directive 2013/34/EU "on the annual financial statements, consolidated financial statements and related reports of certain types of undertakings".

[45] AMLA Regulation, Rec. 5, 19–32, 86, Art. 5(3), Chapter II ("Tasks and Powers of the Authority") Section 3 ("Direct supervision of selected obliged entities"), in particular Art. 16 ("Joint supervisory teams").

[46] AMLA Regulation, Rec. 33, Chapter II ("Tasks and Powers of the Authority") Section 4 ("Indirect supervision of non-selected obliged entities"), in particular Art. 31 ("Coordination and facilitation of the work of the AML/CFT supervisory colleges in the financial sector"), Art. 36 ("Coordination and facilitation of the work of AML/CFT supervisory colleges in the non-financial sector"); 6th AMLD, Art. 49–50.

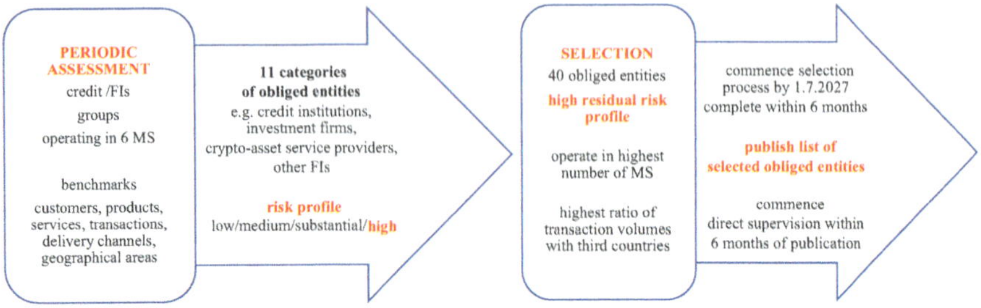

Fig. 3.2 Selection of obliged entities for direct supervision

Table 3.5 Comparison between joint supervisory teams

	SSM Framework Regulation No. 468/2014	**AMLA Regulation 2024/1620**
definition	Art. 2 "joint supervisory team" means a team of supervisors in charge of the supervision of a significant supervised entity/group	
main provision	Art. 3-6	Art. 16 Cf. also Art. 89, 115
supervision of	significant supervised entity/group in participating MS	selected obliged entity
staff members	ECB & NCAs	AMLA & national financial supervisors responsible for supervision of selected obliged entity
JST coordinator assisted by	NCA sub-coordinators	national sub-coordinators
qualification and diversity		sufficient level of knowledge, expertise, experience sufficiently **diverse** knowledge, backgrounds, expertise, experience

By contrast, the term "AML/CFT supervisory college" is expressly defined in Art. 2(8) of the 6th AMLD as "a permanent structure for cooperation and information sharing for the purposes of supervising a group or an entity that operates in a host Member State or third country". Despite resembling "colleges of supervisors" that already exists *de lege lata* under EBA Regulation No. 1093/2010[47] and SSM

[47] Regulation (EU) No. 1093/2010 of the European Parliament and of the Council of 24 November 2010 establishing a European Supervisory Authority (European Banking Authority), OJ L 331, 15.12.2010, p. 12–47 (EBA Regulation).

Framework Regulation No. 468/2014, it is after all a new term that deviates both in form and in substance: Not only can it oversee credit institutions, FIs as well as non-financial obliged entities, also its participants may include non-financial supervisors, third-country counterparts and "additional observers"[48] (see Table 3.6).

Compared with restricted opportunities for third countries to participate in traditional colleges of supervisors or more generally in the work of the EBA and the ECB,[49] the overhauled AML/CFT framework evinces an unprecedented degree of openness and inclusiveness[50]: Third-country counterparts can actively request participation or be invited by members of supervisory colleges,[51] and advisers, experts or "any person whose opinion may be of interest" could theoretically join AMLA's General Board meetings as an observer[52] (see Table 3.7).

To reinforce the effectiveness and consistency of supervisory outcomes, public authorities themselves undergo periodic assessments in the course of which resources, tools and practices are reviewed by their peers and AMLA.[53] The gist for doing so goes beyond suggesting individual follow-up measures: It enables objective comparisons between supervisors in the financial and non-financial sectors alike and captures the degree of supervisory convergence when it comes to practical application and enforcement.[54] In like manner, peer reviews are conducted for FIUs, who—like supervisors—also fall within the remit of AMLA[55] (see Fig. 3.3).

---

[48] 6th AMLD, Art. 49 ("AML/CFT supervisory colleges in the financial sector"), Art. 50 ("AML/CFT supervisory colleges in the non-financial sector").

[49] EBA Regulation No. 1093/2010, Art. 75 ("Participation of third countries"); Directive 2013/36/EU of the European Parliament and of the Council of 26 June 2013 on access to the activity of credit institutions and the prudential supervision of credit institutions and investment firms, OJ L 176, 27.6.2013, p. 338–436 (Capital Requirements Directive), Art. 116 ("Colleges of supervisors"); Basic SSM Regulation No. 1024/2013, Rec. 70, 80, Art. 4 ("Tasks conferred on the ECB"), Art. 8 ("International relations"), Art. 26 ("Supervisory board"); SSM Framework Regulation No. 468/2014, Art. 9 ("ECB as chair of college of supervisors"), Art. 10 ("ECB and NCAs as members of college of supervisors"), Art. 114 ("Investigatory powers pursuant to Art. 10 to 13 SSM Regulation under the regime of close cooperation"), Art. 115 ("Supervision of significant supervised entities in participating Member State in close cooperation").

[50] See also 6th AMLD, Rec. 90, 98 encouraging cross-border cooperation "to the greatest extent possible and regardless of … nature or status" of the supervisors.

[51] 6th AMLD, Art. 49 ("AML/CFT supervisory colleges in the financial sector"), Art. 50 ("AML/CFT supervisory colleges in the non-financial sector").

[52] AMLA Regulation, Art. 62 ("Meetings of the General Board").

[53] AMLA Regulation, Art. 30 ("Assessments of the state of supervisory convergence"), Art. 35 ("Peer reviews").

[54] AMLA Regulation, Section 4 ("Indirect supervision of non-selected obliged entities"), Section 5 ("Oversight of the non-financial sector").

[55] AMLA Regulation, Art. 48 ("Peer review"); 6th AMLD, Rec. 64.

Table 3.6 Comparison between supervisory colleges

	EBA Reg. 1093/2010	**SSM Framework Reg. 468/2014**	**AMLA Reg. 2024/1620**	**6th AMLD 2024/1640**
DEFINITION AND LEGAL BASIS	Art. 1, 8, 21 **college of supervisors** established by legislative acts referred to in Art. 1(2)	Art. 8-10 **college of supervisors** established pursuant to Art. 116 Directive 2013/36/EU or by ECB with NCAs	Rec. 9, Art. 5, 6, 31, 36 AMLA ensure/establish/assist/facilitate **AML/CFT supervisory colleges**	Art. 2 **AML/CFT supervisory college** permanent structure for cooperation and info sharing supervise group/entity that operates in host MS / third country Rec. 90-92, Art. 49, 50 MS ensure AML/CFT supervisory college is set up by financial/non-financial supervisors in charge of parent undertaking / head office
SUPERVISE	cross-border credit/FIs	significant credit institutions (mixed) FHCs parent in participating MS	AML/CFT supervisory colleges in **financial/nonfinancial sector** credit/FIs, (non-selected) obliged entities in nonfinancial sector operate in several (2/3) MS, part of cross-border group	
PERMANENT MEMBERS	EBA staff have full participation rights NCAs	ECB chair/member/participate (Rec. 42, Art. 4 Basic SSM Reg. No. 1024/2013) NCAs	AMLA staff have full participation rights	**financial/non-financial supervisors** in charge of parent undertaking / head office establishments /infrastructure in host MS obliged entity carrying out activities in other MS
OBSERVERS		NCAs where parent/subsidiaries/significant branches/ supervised entities are established	**AMLA** may attend meetings of AML/CFT supervisory colleges facilitate their work, observer status non-financial supervisors of other MS (where non-financial obliged entities provide services) additional observers may be invited / allowed upon request prudential supervisors, ECB, ESAs, FIUs third country counterparts under certain conditions (confidentiality, data protection) (third-country credit/FIs established in 3 MS or Union groups or credit/FIs operate branches/subsidiaries in those third countries)	

Table 3.7 Participation of third parties

AMLA Regulation	
Art. 57 General Board	**Other observers** may be admitted on an ad hoc basis if approved by two-thirds majority of voting members of the General Board
Art. 62 General Board meetings	**advisers or experts** General Board may invite **any person** whose opinion may be of interest to attend as an **observer**
Art. 93 Cross-border partnership for info sharing	Upon unanimous consent of participating members, **other third parties** may be invited to participate, on an occasional basis, in meetings of the partnership, where relevant.
Rec. 82 Art. 95 Cooperation with third countries	AMLA may develop contacts and enter into administrative arrangements with **AML/CFT authorities in third countries** that have regulatory, supervisory and FIU-related competences in field of AML/CFT as well as with **third-country administrations.** AMLA shall have leading role in facilitating interactions between several Union supervisory authorities and FIUs with **third-country authorities**
6th AMLD	
Rec. 43 Art. 12 Access to BO registers for persons with legitimate interest	**obliged entities, FIUs, law enforcement, judicial authorities from third countries** can access BO register following natural/legal persons shall be deemed to have a legitimate interest: (a) persons acting for purposes of **journalism, reporting or media** (b) **civil society organizations**, incl. **NGOs** and **academia** (d) **entities** subject to AML/CFT requirements in third countries (e) **third-country counterparts** of Union AML/CFT competent authorities **any natural/legal person that can demonstrate legitimate interest** has access to BO info
Rec. 77 Art. 30 FIU.net	FIU.net may also be used for communications with **FIUs' counterparts in third countries**
Rec. 82 Art. 32 Joint analysis	FIUs can invite **third parties** to take part in the joint analysis where such participation would fall within mandates of those third parties

(continued)

Table 3.7 (continued)

Rec. 90 Art. 49, 50 AML/CFT supervisory colleges in financial / non-financial sector	set-up of AML/CFT supervisory colleges in non-financial/financial sector obliged entities established in several MS / part of cross-border group **Third-country financial supervisors** can be invited under certain conditions Financial supervisors may allow **counterparts in third countries to participate as observers** in AML/CFT supervisory colleges where third-country credit/FIs established in at least 3 MS or Union groups/credit/FIs, obliged entities in non-financial sector or groups thereof operate branches and subsidiaries in those third countries, provided that: third-country counterparts submit a **request** for participation and members of college agree, or members of college agree to **invite** those third-country counterparts **additional observers** may be invited, provided that confidentiality requirements are complied with. By 10 July 2026, AMLA shall develop draft regulatory technical standards that specify **terms of cooperation with observers, participation of supervisors in third countries**
Rec. 99 Art. 51 Coop. with supervisors in third countries	MS can authorise supervisors to conclude cooperation agreements, exchange confidential info with **counterparts in third countries** in compliance with applicable rules for personal data transfers. AMLA to assess equivalence of professional secrecy requirements applicable to third-country counterpart
Art. 61 Cooperation	competent authorities shall provide BO information to **counterpart competent authorities of third countries** in timely manner and free of charge

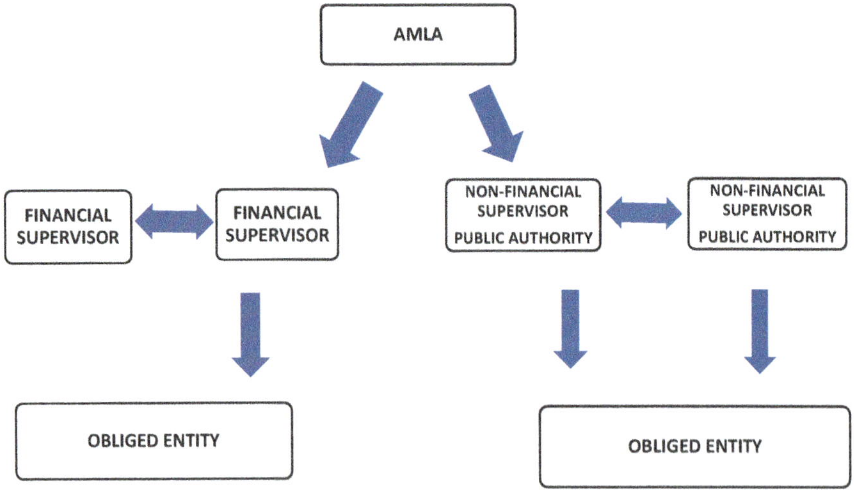

Fig. 3.3 Periodic assessments and peer review

3.3 Cooperation and Information Sharing

This brings us to AMLA's rapport with other actors, which is marked by an overarching precept to cooperate in good faith and to exchange information. Congruent with the principle of sincere cooperation between the Union and Member States enshrined in Art. 4(3) TEU,[56] AMLA, national supervisory authorities and FIUs, too, are bound by a similar duty to assist each other[57] (see Fig. 3.4).

In addition, AMLA will collaborate with non-AML/CFT authorities[58] at the national and supranational level, including EU institutions (e.g. European Commission, ECB), European supervisory authorities[59] (i.e. EBA, ESMA, EIOPA, European Data Protection Supervisor[60]), administrative bodies (i.e. European Anti-Fraud

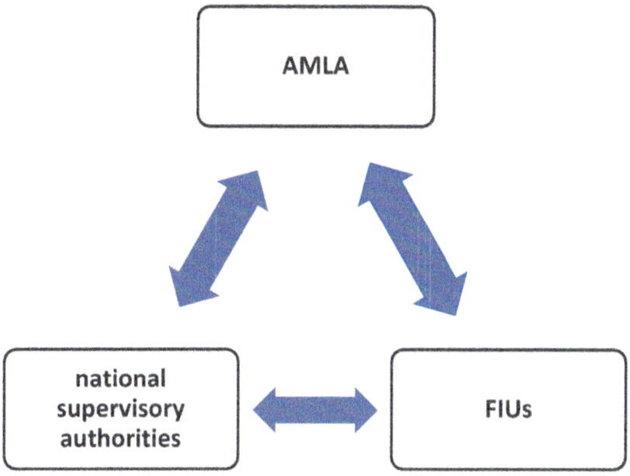

Fig. 3.4 Duty to cooperate and obligation to exchange information

[56] AMLA Regulation, Rec. 27, noting that "relevant actors involved in the application of the AML/CFT framework should cooperate with each other in accordance with the duty of sincere cooperation enshrined in the Treaties".

[57] AMLA Regulation, Rec. 16, 42, Art. 7 ("Cooperation within the AML/CFT supervisory system), Art. 39 ("Cooperation between the Authority and Financial Intelligence Units"). See also 6th AMLD, Art. 23 ("Provision of information to supervisors"), Art. 29 ("Cooperation between FIUs"), Art. 31 ("Exchange of information between FIUs"), Art. 32 ("Joint analyses"), Art. 42 ("Disclosure to FIUs"), Art. 43 ("Provision of information to FIUs"), Art. 44 ("General principles regarding supervisory cooperation"), Art. 45 ("Provision of information on cross-border activities"), Art. 46 ("Provisions related to cooperation in the context of group supervision"), Art. 47 ("Supervisory cooperation regarding obliged entities carrying out cross-border activities"), Art. 48 ("Exchange of information in relation to implementation of group-wide policies in third countries"), Art. 63 ("Cooperation with AMLA"). Cooperation between other authorities is contemplated on numerous occasions as well, see e.g. the 6th AMLD, Art.1(g), Art. 45 ("Provision of information on cross-border activities"), Art. 46 ("Provisions related to cooperation in the context of group supervision").

[58] For a legal definition, see AMLA Regulation, Art. 2(1)(4). See also 6th AMLD, Art. 61 ("General provisions") with reference to policymakers and tax authorities.

[59] AMLA Regulation, Art. 91 ("Cooperation with the European Supervisory Authorities").

[60] AMLA Regulation, Rec. 77, Art. 98 ("Data protection"); AML/CFT Regulation, Rec. 99.

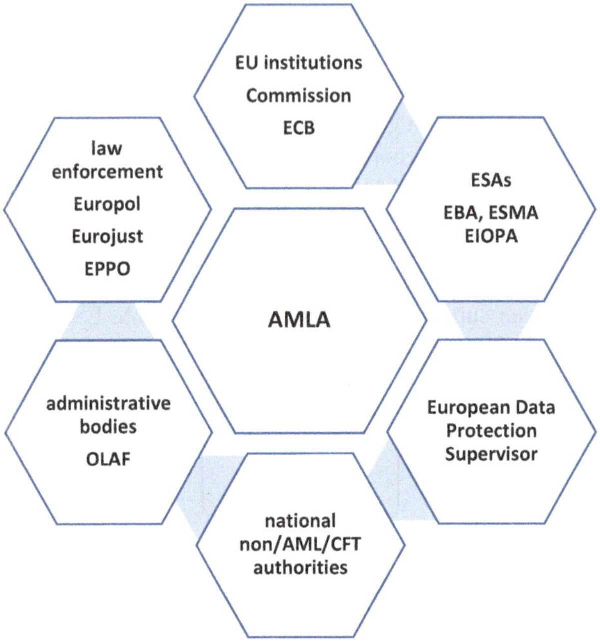

Fig. 3.5 Cooperation with EU and other national authorities

Office [OLAF]) and law enforcement authorities (i.e. European Union Agency for Law Enforcement Cooperation [Europol], Eurojust, European Public Prosecutor's Office [EPPO])[61] (see Fig. 3.5).

Not mandatory but a voluntary option is AMLA's participation in existing "partnerships for information sharing", which obliged entities are entitled to sign with trusted peers who have undergone a data protection impact assessment (European Commission 2024a, p. 10).[62] FIUs and competent authorities may decide to join in the exchange of information, whereby these agreements are transformed into public-private partnerships. Considering the increasing significance of these fora, AMLA may also set up new cross-border partnerships and invite Union bodies, offices, agencies and third parties to take part[63] (see Fig. 3.6 and Table 3.8).

[61] AMLA Regulation, Rec. 79, 81, Art. 41 ("Reporting and transmission of the results of joint analyses"), Art. 91 ("Cooperation with the European Supervisory Authorities"), Art. 92 ("Cooperation with non-AML/CFT authorities"), Art. 94 ("Cooperation with OLAF, Europol, Eurojust and the EPPO").

[62] AMLA Regulation, Rec. 80, Art. 93 ("Partnerships for information sharing in the field of AML/CFT"); AML/CFT Regulation, Art. 75 ("Exchange of information in the framework of partnerships for information sharing"). For a legal definition, see AML/CFT Regulation, Art. 2(1)(57).

[63] AMLA Regulation, Rec. 80, Art. 93 ("Partnerships for information sharing in the field of AML/CFT").

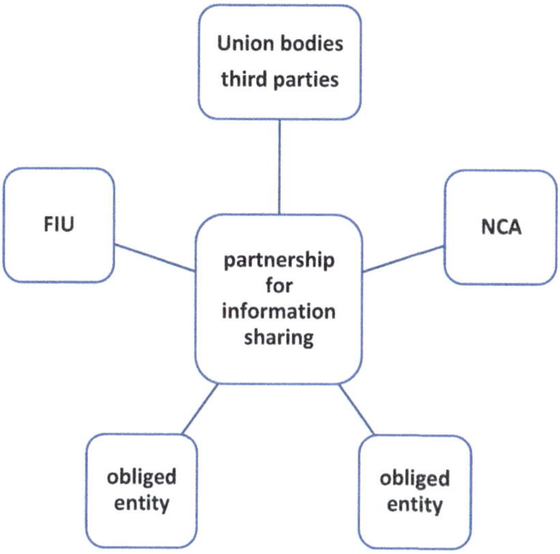

Fig. 3.6 Partnership for information sharing

Table 3.8 Cooperation and exchange of information

PRINCIPLE OF SINCERE COOPERATION, ART. 4(3) TEU		
cooperate with trust/full mutual respect ensure flow of info	DUTY TO COOPERATE IN GOOD FAITH OBLIGATION TO EXCHANGE INFO	
ESFS **EBA & EIOPA & ESMA** **Joint Committee, ESRB**	**SSM** **ECB & NCAs & NDAs**	Art. 7 AML/CFT supervisory system AMLA & national AML/CFT supervisory authorities
Art. 9a **Tasks related to ML/TF** EBA leading/coordinating/monitoring role **EBA &** **competent authorities** **(incl. ECB, supervisory authorities, FIUs)**		Art. 39 Support and coordination mechanism for FIUs AMLA & FIUs FIUs & FIUs
		Art. 92, 94 Cooperation with non-AML/CFT authorities AMLA & ECB, ESAs, NCAs OLAF, Europol, Eurojust, EPPO
EBA Regulation	Basic SSM Regulation SSM Framework Regulation	AMLA Regulation

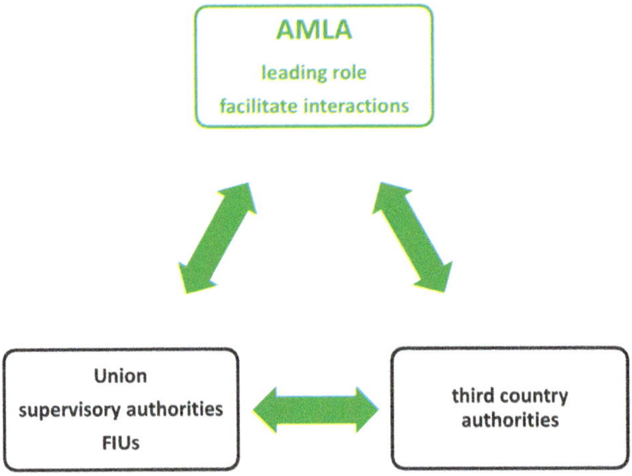

Fig. 3.7 Cooperation with third countries

Vis-à-vis third countries and international organizations, AMLA is authorized to "develop contacts and enter into administrative arrangements."[64] What's more, AMLA is entitled to "develop model administrative arrangements" which "supervisory authorities and FIUs shall make every effort to follow".[65] On top of coordinating joint analyses of cross-border cases,[66] AMLA may even assume "a leading role" in facilitating interactions between EU supervisory authorities, FIUs and third country authorities.[67] This also entails the notion that "FIUs should be encouraged to conclude bilateral agreements and memoranda of understanding with counterparts from third countries", as postulated by the 6th AMLD[68] (see Fig. 3.7).

Conducive for such purposes is the fact that AMLA is designated to manage the AML/CFT database[69] and FIU.net, a secure system for the exchange of financial intelligence information that can also be utilized for communications with

---

[64] AMLA Regulation, Art. 95 ("Cooperation with third countries and international organisations").

[65] AMLA Regulation, Art. 95(2).

[66] AMLA Regulation, Art. 40 ("Conduct of joint analyses"), 6th AMLD, Art. 32 ("Joint analyses").

[67] AMLA Regulation, Art. 95(3).

[68] 6th AMLD, Rec. 75.

[69] AMLA Regulation, Art. 11 ("Central AML/CFT database").

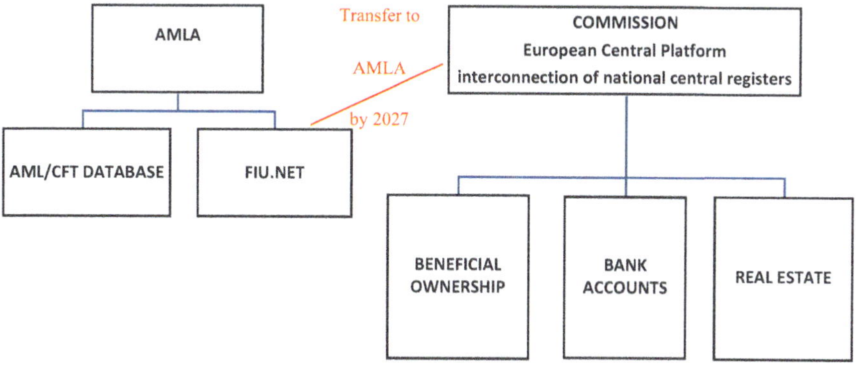

Fig. 3.8 Central databases and registers

third countries.[70] Thanks to the improved interconnection of national central registers through the European Central Platform maintained by the European Commission,[71] a common pool of data pertaining to beneficial ownership,[72] bank accounts (coupled with payment accounts, securities accounts, crypto-asset accounts, safe-deposit boxes)[73] and real estate[74] is another enticing point, last but not least because the 6th AMLD acknowledges that obliged entities, supervisory authorities, FIUs, law enforcement and judicial authorities from third countries (along with journalists, NGOs, academics) "shall be deemed to have a legitimate interest to access" respective information.[75] Such a privilege in favor of third countries must not be taken for granted after a judgment of the European Court of Justice in November 2022 invalidated a provision of the 5th AMLD that granted any member of the general public access to beneficial ownership registers[76] (see Fig. 3.8).

[70] AMLA Regulation, Rec. 9, 52, Art. 5(5)(i), 47 ("FIU.net"); 6th AMLD, Rec. 77, 125 (noting that the Commission should continue to host FIU.net on a temporary basis), Art. 30 ("Protected channels of communication"), Art. 73 ("Transitional management of FIU.net").

[71] 6th AMLD, Rec. 54 and Art. 10 with references to the 5th AMLD and Art. 22 of Directive 2017/1132 establishing the European Central Platform. Rather than replacing national databases, single digital gateways (single access points) will expedite the swift retrieval of reliable sources across the entire EU. The decentralized component of such a centralized mechanism adds an extra layer of protection in the event of a cyberattack or random abuse, thereby making it less prone to falling victim and helping keep personal information safe.

[72] 5th AMLD, Art. 30(10), Art. 31(9); 6th AMLD, Art. 10 ("Central beneficial ownership registers").

[73] 5th AMLD, Art. 32a; 6th AMLD, Rec. 57, Art. 16 ("Bank account registers and electronic data retrieval systems").

[74] 5th AMLD, Art. 32b; 6th AMLD, Art. 18 ("Single access point to real estate information").

[75] 6th AMLD, Rec. 43, Art. 12 ("Specific access rules to beneficial ownership registers for persons with legitimate interest").

[76] Judgment of the Court (Grand Chamber) of 22 November 2022. WM and Sovim SA v Luxembourg Business Registers. Joined Cases C-37/20 and C-601/20.

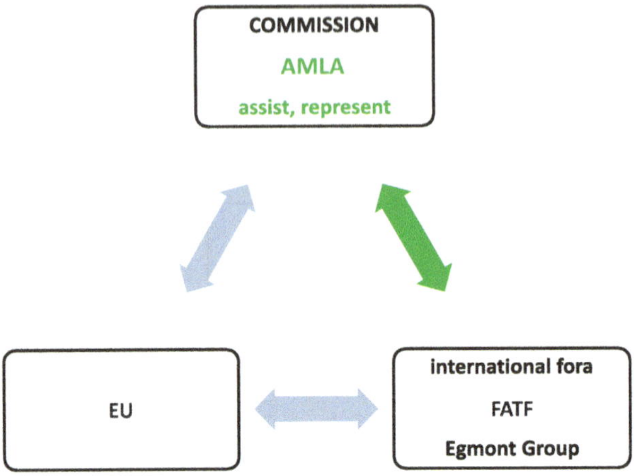

Fig. 3.9 Representation in international fora

Headed by its Chair,[77] AMLA shall thus bolster the "united, common, consistent and effective representation of the Union's interests in international fora", notably by assisting the European Commission, who is a member of the FATF and an observer to the Egmont Group.[78] It will enrich the EU's external delegation team with its expertise and competency and open up new frontiers. In anticpation of such an influential actor, third country administrations should prepare to open new avenues for mutual exchange and cooperation, be it at the bilateral or multilateral level (see Fig. 3.9).

References

Authority for Anti-Money Laundering and Countering the Financing of Terrorism (AMLA) (2024) About AMLA. https://www.amla.europa.eu/about-amla_en. Accessed 2 Dec 2024

European Banking Authority (EBA) (n.d.) Anti-Money Laundering and Countering the Financing of Terrorism. https://www.eba.europa.eu/regulation-and-policy/anti-money-laundering-and-countering-financing-terrorism. Accessed 2 Dec 2024

European Banking Authority (EBA) (2020, February) Factsheet on AML/CFT. https://www.eba.europa.eu/sites/default/documents/files/document_library/News%20and%20Press/Press%20Room/Press%20Releases/2020/EBA%20acts%20to%20improve%20AML/CFT%20supervision%20in%20Europe/AML%20CFT%20Factsheet.pdf

European Commission (2024a, April 24) Questions and Answers: Anti-Money Laundering and Countering Financing of Terrorism (AML/CFT). https://finance.ec.europa.eu/document/download/553ff649-fce8-4e31-b54c-01f562ca0bb3_en?filename=240424-anti-money-laundering-faqs_en.pdf

[77] AMLA Regulation, Art. 3 ("Legal status"), Art. 69 ("Responsibilities of the Chair of the Authority").

[78] AMLA Regulation, Art. 95(4).

European Commission (2024b, April 24) Questions and Answers: the new EU Anti-Money Laundering Authority (AMLA). https://finance.ec.europa.eu/document/download/61cf5a0d-0e5d-43e2-876a-8e68e45c7f1f_en?filename=240424-anti-money-laundering-faqs_en_0.pdf

European Union (EU) (2024, September 23) Preventing abuse of the financial system for money laundering and terrorism purposes (until 2027). https://eur-lex.europa.eu/legal-content/EN/TXT/?uri=legissum%3A230804_1

Kern A (2016) The European Central Bank and Banking Supervision: the regulatory limits of the single supervisory mechanism. Eur Company Financ Law Rev (ECFR) 13(3):467–494. https://doi.org/10.1515/ecfr-2016-5001

Maddaloni A, Scopelliti A (2022) The architecture of supervision and prudential policy. In: Holzmann R, Restoy F (eds) Central banks and supervisory architecture in Europe. Elgar, pp 34–48. https://doi.org/10.4337/9781802208894.00009

Pavlidis G (2024) The birth of the new anti-money laundering authority: harnessing the power of EU-wide supervision. J Financ Crime 31(2):322–330. https://doi.org/10.1108/JFC-03-2023-0059

Schlarb DD (2022) Rethinking anti-money laundering supervision: the single supervisory mechanism - a model for a European anti-money laundering supervisor? New J Eur Crim Law 13(1):69–90. https://doi.org/10.1177/20322844221085949

Van den Broek M (2014) Designing supervision under the preventive anti-money laundering policy in the European Union. Utrecht Law Rev 10(5):151–167. https://doi.org/10.18352/ulr.306

Chapter 4
Substantive Reforms

Abstract This chapter illuminates the substantive features lying at the heart of EU reforms, notably the classification of modern financial intermediaries as obliged entities. Their duty to perform customer due diligence must be perceived in the light of dynamic risk factors. Refined techniques to track the true identities of beneficial owners will make it harder for remote persons to hide behind walls of nominees or other legal arrangements. Third countries will be screened and encounter tailored measures, if they pose a threat to the Union's financial system.

4.1 Obliged Entities

Turning now to the substantive content, the prime question is who should be subject to AML/CFT rules. Under the 4th AMLD, the list of obliged entities expressly covered credit institutions and FIs (insurance undertakings, investment firms), along with six categories of professions susceptible to ML/TF (i.e. accountants and tax advisors, notaries and lawyers, trust or company service providers, estate agents, traders in goods conducting cash transactions of at least EUR 10,000, providers of gambling services including casinos).[1] An open ended clause required Member States to extend the scope of application to other "professions and to categories of undertakings" whose activities "are particularly likely to be used for the purposes of money laundering or terrorist financing".[2]

In 2018, the 5th AMLD for the first time declared "providers engaged in exchange services between virtual currencies and fiat currencies" and "custodian wallet providers" as obliged entities.[3] Slightly departing from the taxonomy of the 5th AMLD – speaking of "virtual currencies" (VCs), the EU nowadays prefers to speak of "crypto-assets", extensively elaborating on them in Regulation 2023/1114 "on

[1] 4th AMLD, Art. 2.

[2] 4th AMLD, Art. 4.

[3] 4th AMLD as amended by the 5th AMLD, Art. 2(1)(3)(g) and (h), Art. 3(18) and (19).

Y. L. A. Chiu, *Money Laundering and Terrorist Financing*,
SpringerBriefs in Law and Regulation & Innovation,
https://doi.org/10.1007/978-981-96-6654-6_4

markets in crypto-assets"[4] (MiCA Regulation),[5] which is a cornerstone of the EU's agenda to promote "Digital Finance" (European Commission 2020). The accommodation of crypto-assets within the EU framework emulates consecutive updates to FATF recommendations in October 2018, June 2019 and June 2021 on new technologies (European Commission 2024a).[6] Hoping to bring "virtual assets" at large within the ambit of AML/CFT standards,[7] the FATF does not confine "virtual asset service providers" (VASPs) to exchanges between virtual assets and fiat currencies or safekeeping but concedes a range of other activities, such as exchanges between one or more forms of virtual assets (FATF 2012, pp. 137–138).

Taking heed of these trends, the EU AML/CFT reform package targets all types of crypto-asset service providers (CASPs) (European Commission 2024b). It broadly defines CASPs in Art. 2(1)(9) AML/CFT Regulation[8] and Art. 3(15) TFR with reference to existing EU laws and treats them as a subcategory of FIs.[9] As such, CASPs are not separaretly labeled as obliged entities,[10] but nevertheless subject to AML/CFT obligations under Art. 3(2) AML/CFT Regulation covering FIs. Alternatively, Art. 3(3)(b) AML/CFT Regulation addressing "independent legal professionals" such as notaries or lawyers could be relevant where transactions carried out on behalf of clients include managing crypto-assets or opening crypto-assets accounts. Looking ahead, the European Commission will keep an eye on crypto-assets and release follow up proposals for related phenomena.[11]

Another controversy for which a compromise could be reached is whether to count crowdfunding service providers[12] as obliged entities. While the Commission's proposal only sought to compensate for a regulatory gap that left some crowdfunding platforms "either unregulated or … subject to diverging regulatory approaches"

---

[4] Regulation (EU) 2023/1114 of the European Parliament and of the Council of 31 May 2023 on markets in crypto-assets, and amending Regulations (EU) No 1093/2010 and (EU) No 1095/2010 and Directives 2013/36/EU and (EU) 2019/1937, OJ L 150, 9.6.2023, p. 40–205 (MiCA Regulation).

[5] MiCA Regulation, Art. 3(1), point 5 ("crypto-assets"), point 15 ("crypto-asset service providers"), point 16 (defining "crypto-asset service").

[6] TFR, Rec. 9, 10.

[7] TFR, Rec. 2, 6, 9–10; AML/CFT Regulation, Rec. 14.

[8] AML/CFT Regulation, Art. 2(1)(9), defines "crypto-asset service provider" with reference to Art. 3(1), point (15) MiCA Regulation. The terms "crypto-asset" and "crypto-asset services" are defined in AML/CFT Regulation, Art. 2(1)(7) and Art. 2(1)(8) with references to Art. 3(1), point (5) and point (16) MiCA Regulation, albeit with some exceptions.

[9] AML/CFT Regulation, Art. 2(1)(6)(i). See also TFR, Rec. 59, pointing out that "the identification of crypto-asset service providers as financial institutions allows for a single consistent set of rules that applies to entities providing both traditional financial services and crypto-asset services."

[10] The European Commission expressly mentioned CASPS as an obliged entity in its draft AML/CFT Regulation, Art. 3(3)(g), which has meanwhile been deleted.

[11] AML/CFT Regulation, Rec. 15.

[12] Crowdfunding service providers are defined in Art. 2(1)(15) AML/CFT Regulation with reference to Regulation (EU) 2020/1503 of the European Parliament and of the Council of 7 October 2020 on European crowdfunding service providers for business, OJ L 347, 20.10.2020, p. 1–49 (ECSP Regulation).

(European Commission 2021a),[13] the final version of Art. 3(3)(h) AML/CFT Regulation captures "all crowdfunding platforms, including those already licensed under Regulation (EU) 2020/1503",[14] as well as crowdfunding intermediaries. This will help dismantle sham campaigns (European Commission 2024c) that are using online platforms as a pretense for TF or other ulterior purposes. A broad application of the AML/CFT Regulation in addition to the safeguards[15] ordained by the ECSP Regulation offers an extra layer of security and should be welcomed (European Commission 2024b).

Raising the bar beyond international benchmarks, the EU moreover seeks to hold responsible investment migration operators who interact with competent authorities of the Member States on behalf of third-country nationals. These "private companies, bodies or persons"[16] wish to "offer intermediation services to third-country nationals seeking to obtain residence rights in a Member State in exchange for any kind of investment, including capital transfers, purchase or renting of property, investment in government bonds, investment in corporate entities, donation or endowment of an activity to the public good and contributions to the state budget".[17] Member States granting these "golden visas" must designate an authority to manage the risks associated with these applicants, among others by checking their individual profiles and sources of wealth, and by publishlishing annual reports on the number of applications received, including the respective countries of origin.[18] However, objectionable and therefore excluded from the scope of the AML/CFT Regulation are "golden passports" or "investor citizenship schemes, which result in the acquisition of nationality in exchange for such investment, … such schemes must be considered as undermining the fundamental status of Union citizenship and sincere cooperation among Member States"[19] (European Parliament 2022a, b).

The revised catalogue of obliged entities ends with "football agents" and "professional football clubs".[20] Since this popular sport could fall prey to ML and corruption (European Commission 2024c), customer due diligence should be carried out "on investors, sponsors, including advertisers, and other partners and counterparties with whom they transact".[21] Accordingly, the list of obliged entities in Art. 3 AML/CFT Regulation henceforth encompasses a total of 15 professional activities, in addition to credit institutions and FIs.

---

[13] European Commission (2021a, Rec. 13). According to ECSP Regulation, Art. 1(2) the regulation does not apply to project owners who are consumers and crowdfunding offers exceeding a threshold of EUR 5 million.

[14] AML/CFT Regulation, Rec. 16.

[15] ECSP Regulation, Rec. 32, Art. 5, Art. 12.

[16] AML/CFT Regulation, Rec. 21.

[17] AML/CFT Regulation, Art. 3(3)(l).

[18] 6th AMLD, Rec. 11, Art. 5 ("Requirements relating to the granting of residence rights in exchange for investment").

[19] AML/CFT Regulation, Rec. 21.

[20] AML/CFT Regulation, Art. 3(3)(n) and (o), referring to transactions with investors, sponsors, football agents or other intermediaries, transactions for purposes of a football player's transfer.

[21] AML/CFT Regulation, Rec. 24–25.

Although the AML/CFT Regulation envisions an exhaustive enumeration of obliged entities, Member States may grant exemptions (e.g. for limited financial activities), if they notify the European Commission in advance,[22] but the European Commission is empowered to either confirm or interdict national exemptions.[23] Conversely, Member States wishing to include additional sectors that are exposed to ML/TF risks must first notify the Commission, who—following an assessment—can propose action at Union level.[24] Obviously, this gives the Commission a chance to preempt national variations and preserve unionwide conformity. All obliged entities will moreover be subject to minimum registration requirements, insofar as necessary for supervisors to identify and adequately supervise them[25] (see Table 4.1).

The rationale for zooming in on these nascent players in the fields of crypto-assets, crowdfunding, investment migration and sports is the fact that they control access to the EU financial system. Aligning these emerging "gatekeepers"[26] with traditional forms of obliged entities goes in the right direction to ensure a level playing field for those doing the same business and facing similar risks. Unlike credit and financial instutions, which must have a location (e.g. branch) within the territorry of the EU,[27] the classification of these financial intermediaries as obliged entities is not accompanied by any geographic attributes. Insofar, all the aforementioned service providers could theoretically be implicated, no matter where they are located.

Nevertheless, it can be inferred that some form of *de facto* minimum contact must be on hand for the EU to establish jurisdiction.[28] The Transfer of Funds Regulation, for instance, only applies to transfers of crypto-assets where at least one of the CASPs has its registered office in the EU.[29] The MiCA Regulation furthermore requires CASPs falling within its purview[30] to have a registered office in an EU Member State and to obtain prior authorization (Chiu 2022, p. 74).[31] In the same vein, European crowdfunding service providers "shall only be provided by legal persons that are established in the Union and that have been authorised as crowdfunding

[22] 4th AMLD, Art. 2(2)–(9); AML/CFT Regulation, Art. 4–6.

[23] AML/CFT Regulation, Rec. 28, Art. 7 ("Prior notification of exemptions").

[24] 6th AMLD, Rec. 6, Art. 3 ("Identification of exposed sectors at national level").

[25] 6th AMLD, Rec. 7–8 (explaining that "all obliged entities act as gatekeepers of the Union's financial system" wherefore they "must develop specific AML/CFT skills to fulfil this task"), Art. 4 ("Requirements relating to certain service providers").

[26] AML/CFT Regulation, Rec. 8.

[27] AML/CFT Regulation, Art. 2(1)(5) and Art. 2(1)(6)(j) allow the head office to be situated within the Union or in a third country.

[28] A range of constellations involving geographical risk factors, non-resident customers or foreign clients, service providers registered or licenced in third countries, financial services provided by EU entities outside European borders, as well as other cross-border activities, transactions and delivery channels all establish relevant points of contacts linking the EU with foreign players.

[29] TFR, Art. 1 ("Subject matter"), Art. 2 ("Scope").

[30] According to MiCA Regulation, Art. 2(1) the scope of application covers persons that are engaged in the issuance of crypto-assets or provide services related to crypto-assets in the Union.

[31] MiCA Regulation, Art. 59.

Table 4.1 Obliged entities

<table>
<tr><th>4th AMLD, as amended by 5th AMLD</th><th>AML/CFT Regulation</th></tr>
<tr><td colspan="2">auditors, external accountants, tax advisors
trust or company service providers</td></tr>
<tr><td colspan="2">estate agents
providers of gambling services</td></tr>
<tr><td>works of art</td><td>cultural goods, high-value goods</td></tr>
<tr><td colspan="2">traders in</td></tr>
<tr><td>goods
cash transactions EUR 10,000 or more</td><td>precious metals/stones
high-value goods</td></tr>
<tr><td></td><td>credit intermediaries for
mortgage and consumer credits
non-financial mixed activity holding companies</td></tr>
<tr><td colspan="2">credit/FIs</td></tr>
<tr><td>exchange services between
virtual/fiat currencies
custodian wallet providers</td><td>CASPs qualify as FIs</td></tr>
<tr><td colspan="2">notaries/independent legal professionals
manage client money/securities/assets, bank/savings/securities accounts</td></tr>
<tr><td></td><td>crypto-assets, crypto-assets accounts</td></tr>
<tr><td></td><td>crowdfunding
service providers / intermediaries</td></tr>
<tr><td></td><td>investment migration operators</td></tr>
<tr><td></td><td>football agents, professional football clubs</td></tr>
<tr><td>open list
(MS shall extend the scope)</td><td>exhaustive list
(MS shall notify additional sectors)</td></tr>
</table>

service providers".[32] Professional football clubs are by definition legal persons who have been "granted a licence and participate(s) in the national football leagues in a Member State".[33] Where investment migration operators assist non-natives to obtain

[32] ECSP Regulation, Art. 3.

[33] AML/CFT Regulation, Art. 2(1)(52) and (53).

residence rights, it lies in the nature of their services that they interact "directly with" competent authorities in the territory of a Member State.[34] Typically, the activitities will therefore be performed in the EU, although the original founder or "mastermind" can actually be located outside the EU. Once falling under the EU's jurisdiction, these obliged entities will bear responsibility, as will be discussed next. It can not serve as a sound excuse to claim that the country of origin does not demand high standards akin to the EU.

4.2 Customer Due Diligence

Whoever qulifies as an obliged entity has to fulfill major duties, beginning with the preparation of "internal policies, procedures and controls" (e.g. conducting business-wide risk assessments,[35] reporting suspicious transactions,[36] retaining records,[37] monitoring compliance with legal requirements,[38] employing qualified staff members[39]).[40] When establishing—and indeed throughout entire—business relationships, a basic responsibility is to perform customer due diligence (CDD)[41] by identifying, verifying and monitoring the customers.[42] Far from being a bureaucratic exercise, obliged entities must grasp the purpose and intended nature of business transactions more generally, pertaining not only to direct customers but also scrutinizing the hidden participation of BOs, politically exposed persons (PEPs), close associates or family members, and whether any of them are subject to financial sanctions.[43]

---

[34] AML/CFT Regulation, Rec. 21, Art. 3(3)(l).

[35] AML/CFT Regulation, Art. 10 ("Business-wide risk assessment").

[36] 4th AMLD as amended by the 5th AMLD, Chapter IV (in particular Art. 33–35); AML/CFT Regulation, Chapter V ("Reporting obligations").

[37] 4th AMLD as amended by the 5th AMLD and Directive 2019/2177, Chapter V ("Data protection, record-retention and statistical data"), in particular Art. 40; AML/CFT Regulation, Chapter VII ("Data protection and record retention").

[38] 4th AMLD as amended by the 5th AMLD and Directive 2019/2177, Chapter VI ("Policies, procedures and supervision"), in particular Art. 46; AML/CFT Regulation, Chapter II ("Internal Policies, procedures and controls of obliged entities"), in particular Art. 11 ("Compliance functions").

[39] AML/CFT Regulation, Art. 11 ("Compliance functions"), Art. 12 ("Awareness of requirements"), 13 ("Integrity of employees").

[40] 4th AMLD, Art. 8; AML/CFT Regulation, Art. 9 ("Scope of internal policies, procedures and controls").

[41] 4th AMLD as amended by the 5th AMLD and Directive 2019/2177, Chapter II ("Customer due diligence"), in particular Art. 10–24; AML/CFT Regulation, Chapter III ("Customer due diligence").

[42] 4th AMLD as amended by the 5th AMLD, Art. 13–14; AML/CFT Regulation, Rec. 51, 69, Art. 20 ("Customer due diligence measures"), Art. 23 ("Timing of the verification of the customer and beneficial owner identity").

[43] AML/CFT Regulation, Rec. 51, 54, Art. 20 ("Customer due diligence measures").

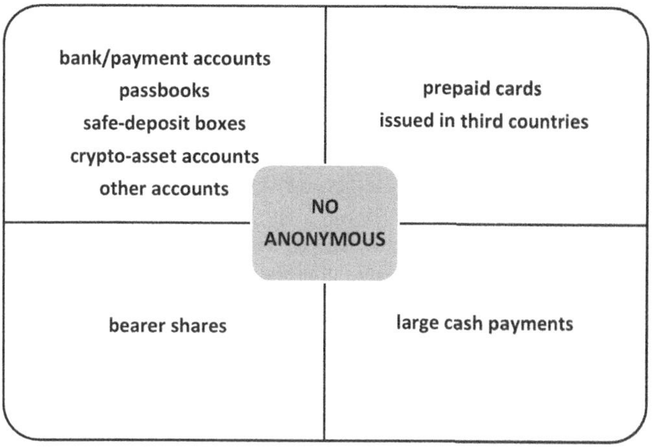

Fig. 4.1 Prohibition of anonymous instruments

Anonymous bank and payment accounts, passbooks and safe-deposit boxes, consequently, are prohibited and subject to CDD.[44] As a general rule, credit institutions and FIs shall for the same reason not accept anonymous prepaid cards issued in third countries,[45] and companies must refrain from issuing bearer shares or bearer share warrants (European Commission 2024a). Anonymous crypto-asset accounts or accounts allowing for the obfuscation of crypto-asset transfers (including through anonymity-enhancing coins) share the same fate[46] (see Fig. 4.1).

In analogy to transfers of funds[47] (i.e. banknotes, coins, scriptural money, electronic money) by payment service providers (PSP), transfers of crypto-assets by CASPs have to conform with Transfer of Funds Regulation 2023/1113 (TFR). Defined in Art. 3(10) TFR,[48] crypto-asset transfers must be accompanied by certain information regarding the originator and the beneficiary to ensure transparency and

[44] AML/CFT Regulation, Art. 79 ("Anonymous accounts and bearer shares and bearer share warrants"). According to Art. 10 of the 4th AMLD, as amended by the 5th AMLD, existing anonymous accounts, passbooks and safe-deposit boxes shall be subject to CDD measures no later than 10 January 2019.

[45] Exemptions are possible, see AML/CFT Regulation, Rec. 58, Art. 79(2).

[46] AML/CFT Regulation, Rec. 160, Art. 79(1).

[47] The term "funds" is specified in TFR, Rec. 3, Art. 3(8), 3(9) with references to Directive 2015/2366 "on payment services in the internal market" and Directive 2009/110/EC "on the taking up, pursuit and prudential supervision of the business of electronic money institutions". A much broader definition is used in AML/CFT Regulation, Art. 2(1)(4), where funds have the same meaning as property described in Directive 2018/1673 "on combating money laundering by criminal law".

[48] TFR, Art. 3(10) defines "transfer of crypto-assets" as "any transaction with the aim of moving crypto-assets from one distributed ledger address, crypto-asset account or other device allowing the storage of crypto-assets to another, carried out by at least one crypto-asset service provider acting on behalf of either an originator or a beneficiary, irrespective of whether the originator and the beneficiary are the same person and irrespective of whether the crypto-asset service provider of the originator and that of the beneficiary are one and the same".

Fig. 4.2 Travel rule. Copyright © FATF/OECD. All rights reserved. The official English of the text, as published on the FATF website, is authoritative

traceability.[49] The originator CASP shall independently verify respective information, whereas the beneficiary CASP should continue to track the transaction.[50] To the extent such information is lacking, the service provider of the beneficiary should make a risk-based decision (e.g. execute, reject, return or suspend that transfer, take appropriate follow-up action)[51] and "report suspicious transactions to the competent authorities".[52] CASPs "shall respond fully and without delay" to enquiries from competent AML/CFT authorities of their home Member State where they have their registered office[53] and keep respective records of information for a certain period of time.[54] The EU has thus aligned itself with the so called "travel rule" (European Commission 2021b, pp. 3–10) enshrined by the FATF in its interpretative note to recommendation 15 on new technologies, urging VASPs to obtain, hold and share information regarding the originators and beneficiaries of virtual asset transfers[55] (see Fig. 4.2).

For the sake of transparency, CDD shall also be mandatory when setting up legal arrangements, creating legal entities, or transferring ownership of legal entities.[56] What's more, certain obliged entities (such as notaries, lawyers, real estate agents, crowdfunding service providers, professional traders) shall apply CDD not only to direct customers but both parties of the transactions, counting in suppliers of goods, merchants, persons seeking or providing funding.[57]

[49] TFR, Rec. 28, Art. 14 ("Information accompanying transfers of crypto-assets").

[50] TFR, Art. 16 ("Detection of missing information on the originator or the beneficiary").

[51] TFR, Art. 17 ("Transfers of crypto-assets with missing or incomplete information on the originator or the beneficiary").

[52] TFR, Rec. 47, Art. 18 ("Assessment and reporting").

[53] TFR, Rec. 52, Art. 24 ("Provision of information").

[54] TFR, Rec. 54, Art. 26 ("Record retention").

[55] TFR, Rec. 2, 6.

[56] AML/CFT Regulation, Art. 19(1)(c).

[57] AML/CFT Regulation, Rec. 60, Art. 19(6).

On top of that, latest reforms cite thresholds for certain transactions: Cash payments made by or to professional traders of goods or service providers for occasional transactions shall have an upper limit of EUR 10,000, whereby Member States may adopt lower limits.[58] Where an occasional cash transaction amounts to EUR 3,000 or more, the customer shall be identified and verified.[59] Transactions carried out by providers of gambling services shall be subject to CDD measures when adding up to EUR 2,000.[60] The same applies to transfers of funds by credit institutions or FIs and transactions carried out by CASPs once they mount up to EUR 1,000, below this cap CASPs shall at least identifty and verify their customers.[61] Under certain conditions, products involving electronic money that are low risk by nature may be exempted from CDD (e.g. the amount stored electronically does not exceed EUR 150)[62] (see Fig. 4.3).

Depending on the intensity of risk, it is possible to deviate from standard due diligence measures[63]: Where a business relationship or transaction presents a lower risk, it may suffice to carry out simplified CDD.[64] Vice versa, enhanced CDD shall be applied in cases of higher risk, especially vis-à-vis third countries with deficient AML/CFT regimes,[65] cross-border correspondent relationships,[66] applicants for residence by investment schemes,[67] PEPs,[68] and wealthy customers holding assets

[58] According to the 4th AMLD, Art. 2(1)(3)(e) professional traders in goods who make or receive cash in an amount of EUR 10,000 or more qualify as obliged entities. Since this has not proven to be effective in preventing ML, this provision shall be replaced by a general prohibition of large cash payments at Union level, notwithstanding certain conditions, exemptions and suspensions. See AML/CFT Regulation, Rec. 18, 161–164, Art. 19(1), Art. 80 ("Limits to large cash payments in exchange for goods or services").

[59] AML/CFT Regulation, Rec. 61, Art. 19 (4).

[60] See also AML/CFT Regulation, Rec. 64, Art. 19 (5).

[61] AML/CFT Regulation, Art. 19(2) and (3).

[62] AML/CFT Regulation, Art. 19(7).

[63] This is possible since 2005, see 3rd AMLD, Rec. 22, 37, 43.

[64] 4th AMLD, Chapter II ("Due diligence"), Section 2 ("Simplified customer due diligence"), as amended by the 5th AMLD and Directive 2019/2177; AML/CFT Regulation, Chapter III ("Customer due diligence"), Section 3 ("Simplified customer due diligence").

[65] AML/CFT Regulation, Art. 36(1) with reference to Art. 29–31.

[66] AML/CFT Regulation, Art. 36 ("Specific enhanced due diligence measures for cross-border correspondent relationships"), Art. 37 ("Specific enhanced due diligence measures for cross-border correspondent relationships for crypto-asset service providers"), Art. 38 ("Specific measures for individual third-country respondent institutions").

[67] AML/CFT Regulation, Rec. 99, Art. 41 ("Specific provisions regarding applicants for residence by investment schemes").

[68] The term "politically exposed person" was first mentioned in the 3rd AMLD, Rec. 25. The circle of PEPs has been enlarged to include public functionaries not only at the international and national, but also at the regional and local level, senior executives in government-controlled enterprises, as well as their family members and close associates. See AML/CFT Regulation, Rec. 90, 91, 92, 93, Art. 2(1)(34), Art. 42 ("Specific provisions regarding politically exposed persons"), Art. 46 ("Family members and persons known to be close associates of politically exposed persons").

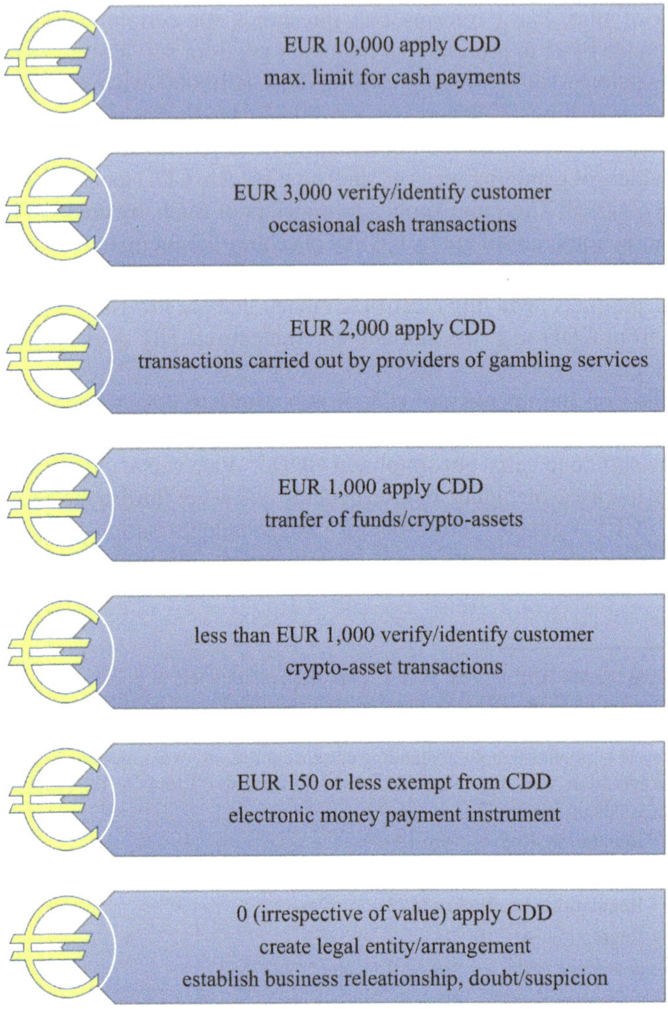

Fig. 4.3 Application of CDD

totalling EUR 50 million.[69,70] Certain relations—notably with shell institutions that have no real physical presence—are absolutely forbidden.[71]

---

[69] AML/CFT Regulation, Rec. 100.

[70] 4th AMLD as amended by the 5th AMLD and Directive 2019/2177, Chapter II ("Customer due diligence"), Section 3 ("Enhanced due diligence"); AML/CFT Regulation, Chapter III ("Customer due diligence"), Section 4 ("Enhanced due diligence").

[71] AML/CFT Regulation, Rec. 80, Art. 39 ("Prohibition of correspondent relationships with shell institutions").

Based on this premise, the intensity of CDD measures to be applied in individual cases varies in accordance with the pinciples of risk-sensitivity and proportionality.[72] Absent a predetermined formula ("one size fits all"), appropriate measures will depend on holistic[73] appraisals of customer risk profiles,[74] the ML/TF risks to which obliged entities are exposed (business-wide risk assessments),[75] national risk assessments of Member States,[76] supranational risk assessments of the European Commission,[77] as well as information provided by international standard setters and other competent authorities[78] (see Fig. 4.4).

Exemplary criteria are enumerated in Annex I ("Indicative list of risk variables"),[79] Annex II ("Lower risk factors")[80] and Annex III ("Higher risk factors").[81] Critical indicators are a customer's professional activity, behaviour and transparency (including BOs,[82] nominees,[83] foreign nationals[84]), the types of products, services, transactions and delivery channels involved,[85] as well as geographic connotations (e.g. country of registration, establishment or residence,[86] main place of business, any other jurisdictions to which the customer has personal links[87]). Called out for the first time as high risk factors are customers owned by legal entities with "no real economic activity, substantial economic presence or apparent economic rationale" in the jurisdiction of their formation, as well as third countries "enabling financial

[72] 4th AMLD as amended by the 5th AMLD, Art. 8, 13–14; AML/CFT Regulation, Rec. 67, 69, 72, 76–80, Art. 9 ("Scope of internal policies, procedures and controls"), Art. 10 ("Business-wide risk assessment"), Art. 16 ("Group-wide requirements").

[73] AML/CFT Regulation, Rec. 152.

[74] 4th AMLD as amended by the 5th AMLD, Art. 13; AML/CFT Regulation, Art. 20 ("Customer due diligence measures"), Art. 26 ("Ongoing monitoring of the business relationship and monitoring of transactions performed by customers").

[75] 4th AMLD, Art. 8; AML/CFT Regulation, Art. 10 ("Business-wide risk assessment"), Art. 16 ("Group-wide requirements").

[76] 4th AMLD, Art. 7 as amended by the 5th AMLD and Directive 2019/2177; 6th AMLD, Art. 8 ("National risk assessment").

[77] 4th AMLD, Art. 6 as amended by the 5th AMLD and Directive 2019/2177; 6th AMLD, Art. 7 ("Risk assessment at Union level").

[78] AML/CFT Regulation, Art. 10(1)(d) and (e).

[79] 4th AMLD as amended by the 5th AMLD, Art. 13; AML/CFT Regulation, Art. 10 ("Business-wide risk assessment"), Art. 20 ("Customer due diligence measures").

[80] 4th AMLD, Art. 16; AML/CFT Regulation, Art. 10 ("Business-wide risk assessment"), Art. 20 ("Customer due diligence measures").

[81] 4th AMLD as amended by the 5th AMLD and Directive 2019/2177, Art. 18; AML/CFT Regulation, Art. 10 ("Business-wide risk assessment"), Art. 20 ("Customer due diligence measures").

[82] AML/CFT, Annex I, para. (a); Annex II, para. (1)(a).

[83] AML/CFT, Annex III, para. (1)(d).

[84] AML/CFT, Annex III, para. (1)(g).

[85] 4th AMLD as amended by the 5th AMLD, Art. 8, Art. 16, Annex II, para. (2), Annex III, para. (2); AML/CFT, Annex I, para. (b) and (c), Annex II, para. (2), Annex III, para. (2).

[86] AML/CFT, Annex II, para. 3; Annex III, para. 3.

[87] AML/CFT, Annex I, para. (a).

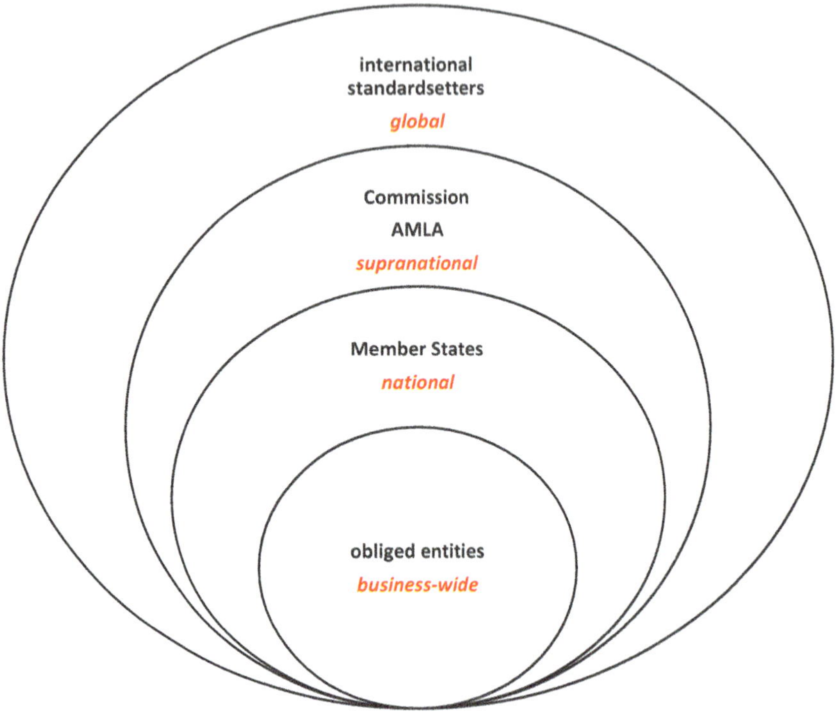

Fig. 4.4 Risk assessments

secrecy" (e.g. those lacking a central beneficial ownership register, obstructing the sharing of information with competent authorities or other jurisdictions).[88]

By contrast, "non-face-to-face business relationships or transactions" have been transferred from Annex III to Annex I in the wake of contemporary reforms, wherefore they no longer count as "potentially higher risks". After all, the EU's Digital Finance Strategy has been promoting a European Digital Identity, in tandem with smart solutions for remote customer identification and authentication ("on-boarding") (European Commission 2024a, p. 7). In total, a dozen risk variables have been added to Annex I, thereby making it conspicuously longer than the previous version, which merely comprises three risk variables focusing on the transaction and business relationship.

Such an array of items that obliged entities must check might be overwhelming and cast doubt on how the provisions of the new framework can achieve proportionality. The problem is exacerbated by the fact that "risk itself is variable in nature, and the variables, on their own or in combination, can increase or decrease the potential risk".[89] There is no easy answer, as the proper level of due diligence inevitably

[88] AML/CFT Regulation, Annex III, para. (1)(h), 1(i), 3(f).

[89] AML/CFT Regulation, Rec. 77.

depends on the circumstances of a particular case. What matters most is for obliged entities to document the formal procedures, how and why a substantive decision was reached in a certain constellation. It is also strongly advised to consult the Commission's regulatory technical standards on CDD,[90] along with AMLA's guidelines ensuring "that the intensity of the monitoring of business relationships and of transactions is adequate and proportionate to the level of risk."[91]

The cost-effectiveness of CDD measures is augmented thanks to the possibility for obliged entities to rely on other obliged entities.[92] The latter can be situated within or outside the EU, as long as they are subject to equivalent requirements and consistent supervision.[93] High-risk third countries, however, are generally precluded, as are third countries with compliance weaknesses and countries that otherwise pose a specific and serious threat to the EU financial system defined in the AML/CFT Regulation.[94] The "(p)rocess of reliance on another obliged entity" and the conditions for transmitting essential information "shall be specified in written agreement between the obliged entities",[95] but "(t)he ultimate responsibility for meeting the customer due diligence requirements shall remain with the obliged entity which relies on another obliged entity".[96] Similar provisions apply in cases of outsourcing AML/CFT related tasks to qualified service providers.[97] The latter may have their location outside the EU but shall "be regarded as part of the obliged entity".[98] The obliged entity shall also notify the supervisor beforehand and "remain fully liable".[99]

In a nutshell, topical reforms put customers from all backgrounds in the spotlight by stretching their definition in multiple directions (encompassing not only direct customers but also beneficiaries and both parties to a transaction), scanning them holistically from myriads of angles according to individual risk profiles (including personal ties and associations), introducing monetary transaction thresholds, barring anonymous products or certain relationships alltogether, and optimizing efficacy by recruiting remote partners via outsourcing and third party reliance (see Fig. 4.5).

---

[90] The regulatory technical standards on CDD should set out the specific simplified measures that obliged entities are able to implement in lower risk situations identified in the risk assessment at Union level conducted by the Commission. When developing draft regulatory technical standards, AMLA is bound to preserve social and financial inclusion, see AML/CFT Regulation, Rec. 78.

[91] AML/CFT Regulation, Rec. 72.

[92] AML/CFT Regulation, Chapter III ("Customer due diligence"), Section 6 ("Reliance on customer due diligence performed by other obliged entities").

[93] 4th AMLD, Art. 26(1); AML/CFT Regulation, Art. 48 ("General provisions relating to reliance on other obliged entities").

[94] 4th AMLD, Art. 26(2); AML/CFT Regulation, 48(4).

[95] AML/CFT Regulation, Art. 49 ("Process of reliance on another obliged entity").

[96] 3rd AMLD, Rec. 27; 4th AMLD as amended by the 5th AMLD, Art. 25–28; AML/CFT Regulation, Rec. 101, Art. 48 48(1).

[97] 3rd AMLD, Rec. 28; 4th AMLD, Rec. 36; AML/CFT Regulation, Rec. 47–50, Chapter II ("Internal policies, procedures and controls of obliged entities"), Section 3 ("Outsourcing").

[98] AML/CFT Regulation, Art. 18 ("Outsourcing").

[99] AML/CFT Regulation, Art. 18 ("Outsourcing").

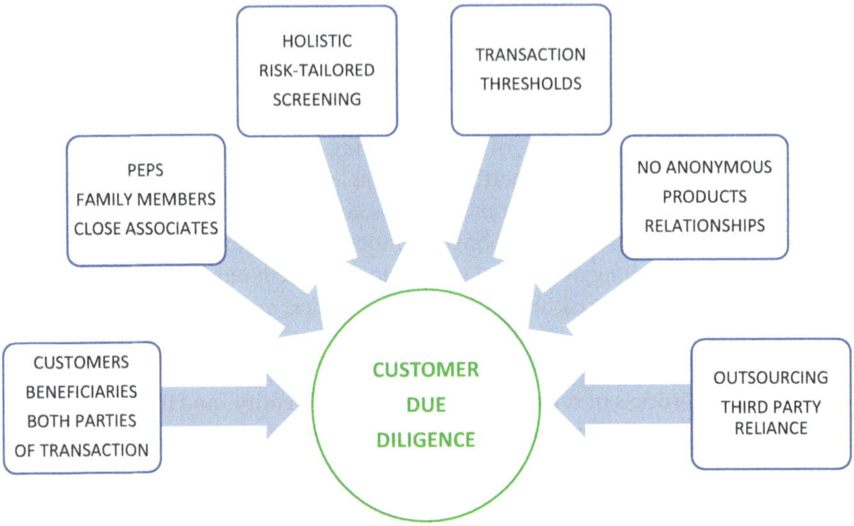

Fig. 4.5 Customer Due Diligence (CDD)

4.3 Beneficial Ownership of Non-EU Citizens

The fundamental duty of CDD is so vital that it must be applied not only directly to formal clients but also indirectly to any BOs. From the outset, this has been postulated in the 1st AMLD,[100] though the term "beneficial owner" (BO) was only later defined in the 3rd AMLD[101] and subsequently modified in the 4th AMLD and 5th AMLD to encompass a wider circle of potential beneficiaries.[102] Hence, the BO can be "any natural person(s) who ultimately owns or controls the customer and/or the natural person(s) on whose behalf a transaction or activity is being conducted".[103]

In corporate entities, a shareholding of more than 25% serves as an indication of ownership or control, although Member States may decide a lower threshold.[104] Alternatively, control can be exercised through voting rights or other means defined in Art. 22(1) to (5) of Directive 2013/34/EU on consolidated financial statements[105] (e.g. right to appoint a majority of management members, right to exercise dominant influence).[106] Should it still be difficult to identify a natural person as BO or in cases

[100] 1st AMLD, Recital, Art. 7.

[101] 3rd AMLD, Rec. 9, Art. 3(6).

[102] See e.g. 4th AMLD, Rec. 12–13.

[103] 4th AMLD as amended by the 5th AMLD, Art. 3(6).

[104] 4th AMLD, Art. 3(6)(a)(i). See also 4th AMLD as amended by the 5th AMLD, Art. 65(3).

[105] Directive 2013/34/EU of the European Parliament and of the Council of 26 June 2013 on the annual financial statements, consolidated financial statements and related reports of certain types of undertakings, OJ L 182, 29.6.2013, p. 19–76.

[106] 4th AMLD, Art. 3(6)(a)(i).

of doubt, "a senior managing official" shall be reported.[107] In the event of trusts and "legal entities such as foundations", natural persons who hold certain positions (e.g. trustee) or exercise "ultimate control … by means of direct or indirect ownership or by other means"[108] are desginated as BOs.[109]

This raises the question how obliged entities can be impelled to execute their CDD duties when true beneficiaries are overseas. Presumably, one can not count on potential perpetrators and their affiliates to reveal their secret alliances on their own. The opposite is to be anticipated: It is probable that they will defy legal obligations and hardly be deterred by sanctions. Even the capability of national supervisors to check, verify and eventually to remove, ban and disassociate unsuitable managers or BOs (e.g. persons convicted of ML; persons lacking good repute, honesty, integrity, knowledge or expertise)[110] does not eliminate the contingency that very important persons (VIPs) will have a host of duly skilled proxies in place, who are ready to act on their behalf without being the true BOs. What is more, peer-to-peer transactions conducted via distributed networks in the absence of structured management (Chiu 2022, pp. 75–76) fail to have an obliged entity who could inquire about the existence of BOs.

All the more commendable are ongoing endeavours to unmask hidden beneficiaries, utilizing a combination (FATF 2012, p. 93) of advanced tactics. Chapter 1 ("General provisions") of the AML/CFT Regulation thus proclaims "beneficial ownership transparency requirements for legal entities, express trusts and similar legal arrangements" as a core subject matter.[111] The hitherto complex definition for "beneficial owner" is reduced in Art. 2(1)(28) AML/CFT Regulation to a general description ("any natural person who ultimately owns or controls a legal entity or an express trust or similar legal arrangement"[112]) and further expounded in Chapter IV ("Beneficial ownership transparency") (see Fig. 4.6).

There, Art. 51 AML/CFT Regulation supplements a refined mechanism to detect the real owners of legal entities.[113] The first overriding criterion is having direct or indirect ownership interest of 25% or more of the shares or voting rights.[114] This threshold will be reassessed in the future and can also be lowered by the European

[107] 4th AMLD, Art. 3(6)(a)(ii).

[108] See also AML/CFT Regulation, Rec. 117, Art. 58 ("Identification of beneficial owners for express trusts and similar legal arrangements").

[109] 4th AMLD as amended by the 5th AMLD, Art. 3(6)(b), 3(6)(c), Art. 31. See in this context Snijder-Kuipers (2023, p. 7), noting that the 25% threshold for legal entities does not apply to trusts, whose BOs are more broadly defined.

[110] 6th AMLD, Art. 6 ("Checks on the senior management and beneficial owners of certain obliged entities").

[111] AML/CFT Regulation, Art. 1 ("Subject matter").

[112] According to AML/CFT Regulation, Art. 2(1)(32) "'legal arrangement' means an express trust or an arrangement which has a similar structure or function to an express trust, including fiducie and certain types of Treuhand and fideicomiso".

[113] AML/CFT Regulation, Art. 51 ("Identification of beneficial owners for legal entities").

[114] AML/CFT Regulation, Art. 52 ("Beneficial ownership through ownership interest").

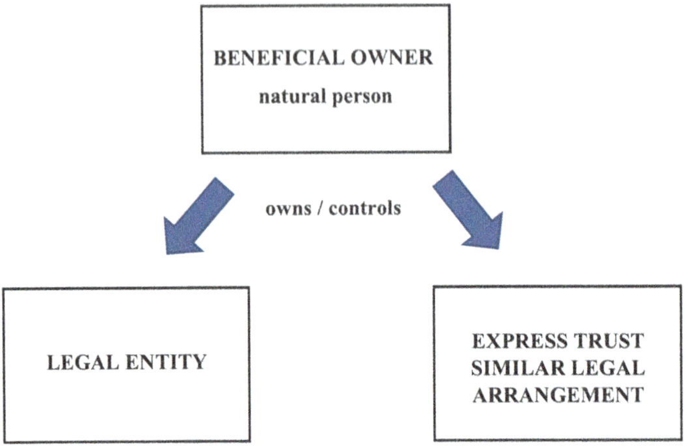

Fig. 4.6 General definition of beneficial owner

Commission to 15%.[115] Following further negotations, the European Commission has been empowered to adopt guidelines "setting out how rules to identify the beneficial owners in different scenarios are to be applied, including through the use of case examples."[116]

The other overriding criterion is control (i.e. "the possibility to exercise, directly or indirectly, significant influence and impose relevant decisions within the legal entity"), either through ownership interest or via other means.[117] The former is satisfied where one owns "50% plus one of the shares or voting rights or other ownership interest", conveying that there is no fix percentage.[118] Based on a multi-pronged approach, control can finally be exercised via other means,[119] such as decision or veto rights, voting arrangements, nominee arrangements, informal agreements, or family relationships.[120] No doubt, this could implicate a vast number of people from all walks of life (see Table 4.2).

BOs of "legal entities similar to express trust" (i.e. foundations) or "express trusts and similar legal arrangements" are designated in Art. 57 and 58 AML/CFT

[115] AML/CFT Regulation, Rec. 107, Art. 52(2), 88 ("Reports"). See in this context also (FATF 2012, pp. 67, 93), citing the 25% threshold only as an example.

[116] AML/CFT Regulation, Rec. 105. See also AML/CFT Regulation, Rec. 135, empowering the Commission to adopt delegated acts and guidelines to enforce beneficial ownership requirements.

[117] AML/CFT Regulation, Art. 53 ("Beneficial ownership through control").

[118] AML/CFT Regulation, Art. 53(2)(c).

[119] AML/CFT Regulation, Rec. 110, noting that "(c)ontrol can generally be exercised by any means, including legal and non-legal means."

[120] AML/CFT Regulation, Art. 53(3) and (4).

Table 4.2 Beneficial owner of legal entity

BENEFICIAL OWNER **natural person**		
direct/indirect **OWNERSHIP** interest	direct/indirect **CONTROL** significant influence	
	ownership interest	**via other means**
15% - **25%** shares / voting rights	50% + 1 shares / voting rights other ownership interest	majority of voting rights right to appoint/remove majority board members decision/veto rights formal/informal agreements voting/nominee arrangements family relations

Regulation with references to natural persons who belong to certain classes (e.g. beneficiaries) or exercise direct or indirect control[121] (see Table 4.3).

De lege ferenda, the European Commission is moreover empowered to promulgate a list of national entities and arrangements that should be subject to the same beneficial ownership transparency requirements as express trusts. Where neither ownership nor control are conclusive, the *ultima ratio* is to name "a senior managing official" instead of the BO. Compared with the *status quo* under the 4th AMLD,[122] this back-up solution will no longer be limited to corporations but be available for all legal entities.[123]

The duty of obliged entities to understand the "ownership and control structure" of their customers, including the existence of any BOs,[124] goes hand in hand with a duty of precisely those persons (i.e. legal entities, trustees, persons holding equivalent positions, BOs) to disclose their status and provide "adequate, accurate

[121] See also AML/CFT Regulation, Rec. 117, Art. 57 ("Identification of beneficial owners for legal entities similar to express trust"), Art. 58 ("Identification of beneficial owners for express trusts and similar legal arrangements").

[122] 4th AMLD, Art. 3(6)(a)(ii).

[123] AML/CFT Regulation, Rec. 113 (referring to "associations, trade unions, political parties or churches"), Rec. 125 (acknowledging the possibility for "senior managing officials to be reported instead of the beneficial owners … Although they are identified in these situations, the senior managing officials are not the beneficial owners"), Art. 22(2), 63(4), 64(4).

[124] 4th AMLD as amended by the 5th AMLD, Art. 13, Art. 14, Chapter III ("Beneficial ownership information"); AML/CFT Regulation, Art. 20(1)(b).

Table 4.3 Comparison between "legal entity similar to express trust" and "express trusts and similar legal arrangements"

BENEFICIAL OWNER natural person	
LEGAL ENTITY SIMILAR TO EXPRESS TRUST (e.g. foundation)	**EXPRESS TRUSTS AND SIMILAR LEGAL ARRANGEMENTS**
founders	settlors
members of management body in its management function	trustees
members of management body in its supervisory function	protectors
beneficiaries	
any other natural person who controls directly/indirectly	any other natural persons exercising ultimate control by means of direct/indirect ownership or other means incl. through chain of control or ownership

and up-to-date" beneficial ownership information.[125] Whereas the aforementioned already applies under existing law,[126] unparalleled notification requirements have been devised for nominees and foreign entities to add efficacy: Pursuant to Art. 66 AML/CFT Regulation nominee shareholders and nominee directors of legal entities shall declare their nominator and the nominator's BO(s) so that this information can be collected in a central register.[127]

By the same token, Art. 67 AML/CFT Regulation ("Foreign legal entities and foreign legal arrangements") stipulates that foreign legal entities, express trusts or similar legal arrangements incorporated or administered outside the Union shall file their beneficial ownership information in a central register when entering into a business relationship with an obliged entity, acquiring real estate or "certain high-value goods"[128] (i.e. jewelry or watches whose value exceeds EUR 10,000, luxury motor vehicles, aircraft or watercraft having a price exceeding EUR 250,000 or EUR

[125] AML/CFT Regulation, Art. 62–64.

[126] 4th AMLD as amended by the 5th AMLD, Art. 30, 31.

[127] AML/CFT Regulation, Rec. 131, Art. 66 ("Nominee obligations").

[128] AML/CFT Regulation, Rec. 166 (noting that "this Regulation introduces for the first time at Union level mandatory threshold-based disclosures in relation to certain high-value goods"), Art. 2(1), point (54) (referring to the goods listed in Annex IV).

Fig. 4.7 Duty to understand and duty to disclose

7,500,000 respectively) in the Union, and when they are awarded a public procurement for goods, services or concessions. The term "business relationship" as defined in Art. 2(1)(19) AML/CFT Regulation merely requires contact between a customer and the professional activities of an obliged entity that is expected to be repeated or of duration. The lack of formal requirements is reasonable, as the parties could otherwise evade their obligations by abstaining from a written agreement. This way construing the registration of beneficial ownership information as a precondition[129] for the validity of the business relationship could be a convincing argument for participants to meet legal expectations (see Fig. 4.7).

To ensure that beneficial ownership registers remain "accurate, adequate and up-to-date", obliged entities may not solely rely on them as a primary source of information.[130] To the contrary, obliged entities should independently collect the essential data they need, either from the customers themselves or by taking recourse to other public resources.[131] Where an obliged entity discovers discrepancies or finds information in the beneficial ownership register to be incorrect, it shall ask the customer to submit correct information and/or report the discrepancy to the entity in charge of the central register.[132] The latter are vested with ample powers, for instance to request necessary information and documents, to conduct inspections at business premises, to withhold or suspend certifications of registrations, and to impose sanctions.[133] This

[129] AML/CFT Regulation, Rec. 55, 132, 133; 6th AMLD, Rec. 44.

[130] AML/CFT Regulation, Rec. 54.

[131] AML/CFT Regulation, Art. 22 ("Identification and verification of the identity of customers and beneficial owners").

[132] AML/CFT Regulation, Art. 24 ("Reporting of discrepancies with information contained in beneficial ownership registers").

[133] 6th AMLD, Rec. 27–31, Art. 10 ("Central beneficial ownership registers").

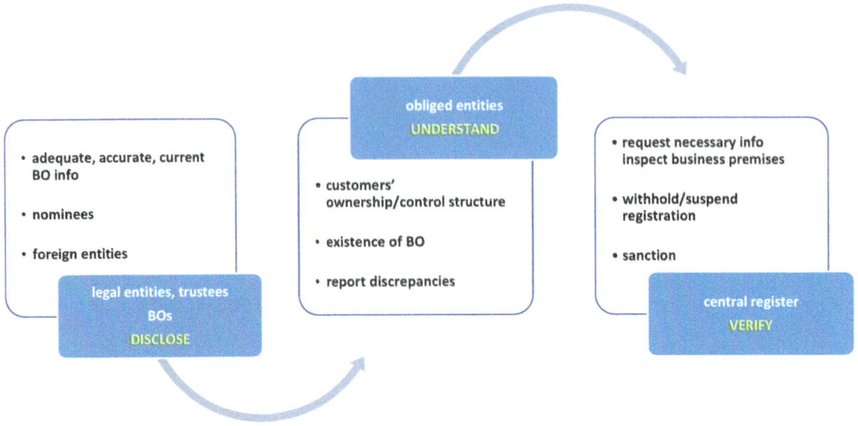

Fig. 4.8 Disclose, understand and verify beneficial ownership information

sort of vigorous cross-checking with the assistance of various information channels[134] and automated data processing maximizes positive synergies and promises to be a powerful remedy in the international arena (see Fig. 4.8).

4.4 Threats Originating from Third Countries

With rising "threats from outside the Union", unprecedented policies targeting third countries and external threats have been formulated.[135] Distinguishing three categories of countries, the AML/CFT Regulation lays out a meticulous approach for early screening with tailored consequences:

"(H)igh-risk third countries" with "significant strategic deficiencies" in their national AML/CFT regimes are subject to "call for action" by international standard-setters.[136] Owing to their "persistent nature" and lack of mitigating measures,[137] they shall be subject to a *potpourri* of "enhanced customer due diligence"[138] and "specific countermeasures"[139] by obliged entities (e.g. systematic reporting of financial transactions; limitation of business relationships or transactions with natural persons or legal entities from those third countries) and/or the Member States

134 AML/CFT Regulation, Rec. 121.

135 AML/CFT Regulation, Chapter III ("Customer due diligence"), Section 2 ("Third-country policy and money laundering and terrorist financing threats from outside the Union").

136 AML/CFT Regulation, Rec. 84, Art. 29 ("Identification of third countries with significant strategic deficiencies in their national AML/CFT regimes").

137 AML/CFT Regulation, Rec. 84, Art. 29(2)(c).

138 AML/CFT Regulation, Art. 34 ("Scope of application of enhanced due diligence measures"). See also 4th AMLD as amended by the 5th AMLD and Directive 2019/2177, Art.18, 18a.

139 AML/CFT Regulation, Art. 35 ("Countermeasures to mitigate money laundering and terrorist financing threats from outside the Union"). The same measures are described in the 4th AMLD as amended by the 5th AMLD, Art. 18a(2)–(3) as "additional mitigating measures".

(e.g. refusing the establishment of subsidiaries, branches or representative offices; more stringent supervisory examination or external audit requirements). They are identified by the European Commission in delegated acts (European Commission 2022),[140] whereby the time to do so has been shortened from one month[141] to 20 days.[142] Given the need for "quick and continuous adaptations", latest reforms require the Commission to review and where necessary to update the delegated acts by adding "necessary countermeasures" upon receiving the notification of a Member State that it has identified a specific risk stemming from a third country and imposed additional countermeasures.[143]

In comparison, third countries that are committed to address "compliance weaknesses" in their legal and institutional framework or effectiveness of implementation are frequently under "increased monitoring" by international organizations and standard setters such as the FATF.[144] They too shall be pinpointed in delegated acts adopted by the Commission and be subject to "specific enhanced due diligence measures" that are commensurate to the particular risk emanating from that country[145] (see Table 4.4).

Table 4.4 Difference between third countries with significant strategic deficiencies and third countries with compliance weaknesses

THIRD COUNTRIES	SIGNIFICANT STRATEGIC DEFICIENCIES	COMPLIANCE WEAKNESSES
designated as	high-risk third countries call for action	increased monitoring
criteria	legal/institutional AML/CFT framework	
	effectiveness of third country's AML/CFT system	
	persistent nature, lack of commitment	commitment to address weaknesses
Commission	delegated acts	
	enhanced DD measures specific **countermeasures**	**specific enhanced** DD measures

[140] See in this context also AML/CFT Regulation, Rec. 83, 167 (with reference to Art. 290 TFEU), Art. 29 ("Identification of third countries with significant strategic deficiencies in their national AML/CFT regimes"), Art. 85 ("Exercise of the delegation").

[141] 4th AMLD as amended by the 5th AMLD, Art. 9.

[142] AML/CFT Regulation, Rec. 84, Art. 29(2).

[143] AML/CFT Regulation, Rec. 84, Art. 29 (6) and (7).

[144] AML/CFT Regulation, Rec. 85, Art. 30 ("Identification of third countries with compliance weaknesses in their national AML/CFT regimes").

[145] AML/CFT Regulation, Rec. 85, Art. 30(2) and (4).

Third countries which otherwise "pose a specific and serious threat to the financial system of the Union and the proper functioning of the internal market" without being subject to calls for actions or increased monitoring by international standard setters can be identified in delegated acts adopted by the European Commission when it is "indispensable" to do so.[146] Like for all third country policies, decisive criteria are the legal and institutional AML/CFT framework, along with its effectiveness. The former is specified "in particular" with regard to criminalization of ML and TF, CDD measures, record-keeping and reporting requirements, as well as the availablity of accurate and timely BO information of legal persons and arrangements. In addition, attention is drawn to the powers and procedures of competent authorities, including effective, proportionate and dissuasive sanctions, as well as the practical cooperation and exchange of information with competent authorities in EU MS. It is worth noting that these criteria are identical with those strategic deficiencies enumerated in Art. 9(2) of the 4th AMLD as amended by the 5th AMLD. A novel aspect is that AMLA may be requested to weigh the "impact on the integrity of the Union's financial system".[147] Should AMLA in its opinion believe that the European Commission should identify the third country as posing a specific and serious threat, the European Commission would have to cite a justification for not doing so.[148] Depending on whether the threat amounts to a "significant strategic deficiency" or "compliance weakness", the European Commission will either identify "specific countermeasures" or "specific enhanced due diligence measures" as mentioned in the foregoing paragraphs. The methodology for dealing with these "exceptional cases"—including the process for interacting with such third countries (European Commission 2024a)—shall be set out in an implementing act of the European Commission[149] (see Table 4.5).

Apart from these country-specific evaluations that are reviewed on a regular basis in terms of proportionality and risk adequacy, the European Commission shall draw up a comprehensive report on supranational risks affecting the entire Union as a whole.[150] The findings underscore the nature and level of ML/TF risks associated with certain exposed areas and sectors of the internal market, prevailing techniques "used in transactions between Member States and third countries", "risks deriving from foreign legal persons and foreign legal arrangements"[151] and, last but not least, comprise recommended measures for EU Member States. The frequency for updating the report has been extended from two[152] to four years, or "more frequently if appropriate".[153]

---

146 AML/CFT Regulation, Rec. 86, Art. 31 ("Identification of third countries posing a specific and serious threat to the Union's financial system").

147 AML/CFT Regulation, Art. 31(3).

148 AML/CFT Regulation, Art. 31 (4).

149 AML/CFT Regulation, Rec. 87, Art. 31 (9).

150 6th AMLD, Art. 7 ("Risk assessment at Union level").

151 6th AMLD, Art. 7 ("Risk assessment at Union level").

152 4th AMLD as amended by the 5th AMLD and Directive 2019/2177, Art. 6.

153 6th AMLD, Art. 7(2).

Table 4.5 Third countries posing a specific and serious threat

THIRD COUNTRIES POSING A SPECIFIC AND SERIOUS THREAT TO UNION'S FINANCIAL SYSTEM		
criteria	legal/institutional AML/CFT framework, in particular criminalization of ML and TF, CDD measures, record-keeping / reporting requirements BO information of legal persons/arrangements	
	effectiveness of third country's AML/CFT system	
	powers/procedures of competent authorities effective/proportionate/dissuasive sanctions cooperation/exchange of information with competent authorities in EU MS	
Commission	delegated acts	
	significant strategic deficiency > specific **countermeasures**	compliance weakness > **specific enhanced** DD measures

The incentives for outlying jurisdictions to keep in step with EU benchmarks are prevalent, given an extensive definition of the term "third countries" in Art. 2(1)(21) AML/CFT Regulation: Aside from "independent state(s)", "any jurisdiction … or autonomous territory that is not part of the Union and that has its own AML/CFT legislation or enforcement regime" is counted. Such a pragmatic delineation is imperative to maximize the cogency of the EU AML/CFT regime. For instance, even where it is contentious whether an autonomous territory qualifies as an independent state (e.g. Taiwan), it would be considered a third country for AML/CFT purposes and as such should take precautions to comply with legal provisions. Seen from this aspect, perceivable signals are being transmitted from the EU to other continents. They could even be a stepping stone and induce others to follow suit, thereby boosting widespread acceptance of international AML/CTF recommendations, which by themselves are not technically binding and contingent on the good will of sovereign states.

References

Chiu YLA (2022) The Euro @20: lessons for the next generation of virtual currencies. Eur Bus Law Rev 33(1):57–85. https://doi.org/10.54648/eulr2022002

European Commission (2020, September 24) Communication on a Digital Finance Strategy for the EU. https://eur-lex.europa.eu/legal-content/EN/TXT/?uri=CELEX:52020DC0591

European Commission (2021a, July 20) Proposal for a regulation on the prevention of the use of the financial system for the purposes of money laundering or terrorist financing. https://eur-lex.europa.eu/legal-content/EN/TXT/?uri=CELEX%3A52021PC0420

European Commission (2021b, July 20). Proposal for a regulation on information accompanying transfers of funds and certain crypto-assets (recast). https://eur-lex.europa.eu/legal-content/EN/TXT/?uri=CELEX%3A52021PC0422

European Commission (2022, January 7) Commission Delegated Regulation 2022/229 amending Delegated Regulation 2016/1675 supplementing Directive 2015/849. https://eur-lex.europa.eu/legal-content/EN/TXT/?uri=CELEX:32022R0229

European Commission (2024a, April 24) Questions and Answers: Anti-Money Laundering and Countering Financing of Terrorism (AML/CFT). https://finance.ec.europa.eu/document/download/553ff649-fce8-4e31-b54c-01f562ca0bb3_en?filename=240424-anti-money-laundering-faqs_en.pdf

European Commission (2024b, April 24) Factsheet: Stronger EU rules to fight financial crime. https://finance.ec.europa.eu/financial-crime/amla/stronger-eu-rules-fight-financial-crime_en

European Commission, Directorate-General for Financial Stability, Financial Services and Capital Markets Union (2024c, April 24) Anti-Money Laundering [Newsletter]. https://finance.ec.europa.eu/news/anti-money-laundering-2024-04-24_en

European Parliament (2022a, February 15) MEPs call for a ban on 'golden passports' and EU rules for 'golden visas' [Press release]. https://www.europarl.europa.eu/news/en/press-room/20220211IPR23114/meps-call-for-a-ban-on-golden-passports-and-eu-rules-for-golden-visas

European Parliament (2022b, March 9) Resolution of 9 March 2022 with proposals to the Commission on citizenship and residence by investment schemes (2021/2026(INL)). https://www.europarl.europa.eu/doceo/document/TA-9-2022-0065_EN.pdf

FATF (2012, updated February 2025) International Standards on Combating Money Laundering and the Financing of Terrorism & Proliferation – The FATF Recommendations. https://www.fatf-gafi.org/en/publications/Fatfrecommendations/Fatf-recommendations.html. Copyright © FATF/OECD. All rights reserved. The official English of the text, as published on the FATF website, is authoritative

Snijder-Kuipers B (2023) Navigating the anti-money laundering landscape – the role companies play in protecting the financial system. IBFD - Fin Capital Markets 24(4). https://www.ibfd.org/sites/default/files/2024-01/selected-journal-articles-ibfd-fcm-aml-2.pdf

Chapter 5
Case Study: Taiwan

Abstract This chapter supplements a case study using the Republic of China (Taiwan) as a concrete example. A founding member of the Asia/Pacific Group on Money Laundering (APG) since 1997 and longstanding member of the Egmont Group since 1998, this Asian pioneer nation has shown notable resilience on its path of adhering to international AML/CFT standards. As such, it merits a closer look and even serves as a model to demonstrate various degrees of assimilation with western concepts. A comparative analysis of the legal framework evidences that Taiwan today has many provisions akin to those of the EU.

5.1 Overview

Supplementing the above discourse, the practical implications of EU reforms shall be illustrated using a concrete case study on the Republic of China (Taiwan). This Asian pioneer merits a closer analysis for several reasons: It was the first jurisdiction in Asia to craft a dedicated Money Laundering Control Act (MLCA)[1] in 1996 (AMLO 2018, p. 5; Lee 1996, p. 212) and is a founding member of the Asia/Pacific Group on Money Laundering (APG) since 1997 (APG 2024), as well as a member of the Egmont Group since 1998 (Egmont Group 2024). The financial intelligence unit (FIU) set up within the Ministry of Justice Investigation Bureau (MJIB) was named Money Laundering Prevention Center (MLPC) and renamed the Anti-Money Laundering Division (AMLD) in 2007 (MJIB 2017a, 2023, p. 3).

The legal and institutional framework kept evolving, as a Counter-Terrorism Financing Act[2] was promulgated in 2016 and a specialized Anti-Money Laundering Office (AMLO) inaugurated under the Executive Yuan (i.e. the executive branch of the government) in 2017. The hope was to better monitor and coordinate nation-wide policies in preparation for the third round of mutual evaluations by APG in

[1] The original title in Chinese is 洗錢防制法, available at the Laws & Regulations Database of the Republic of China (Taiwan) at https://law.moj.gov.tw/LawClass/LawAll.aspx?pcode=G0380131.

[2] The original title in Chinese is 資恐防制法, available at the Laws & Regulations Database of the Republic of China (Taiwan) at https://law.moj.gov.tw/LawClass/LawAll.aspx?pcode=I0030047.

Y. L. A. Chiu, *Money Laundering and Terrorist Financing*,
SpringerBriefs in Law and Regulation & Innovation,
https://doi.org/10.1007/978-981-96-6654-6_5

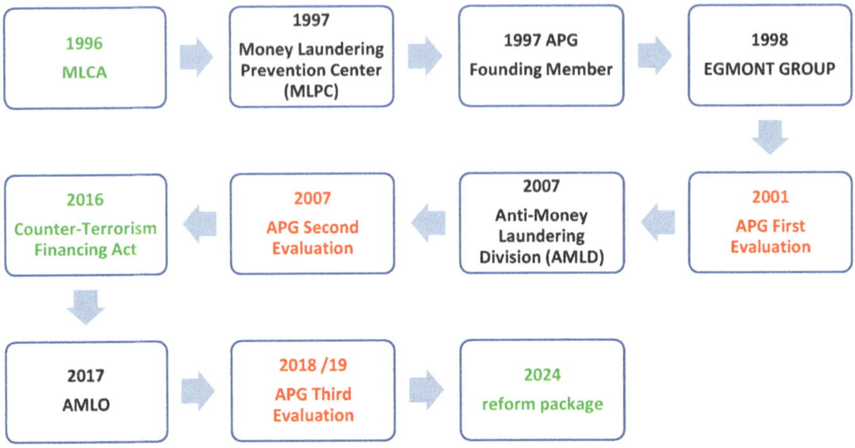

Fig. 5.1 Overview of developments in Taiwan

November 2018 (AMLO 2017, 2018, p. 3). The ratings assigned by APG to "Chinese Taipei" reflect the democratic island nation's resilience, being overall positive in 2001, noncompliant with 11 recommendations in 2007, and—following a transitional follow-up period—compliant, largely compliant or at least partially compliant with all 40 FATF recommendations in 2018 (APG 2007, pp. 198–205; 2019, pp. 22–26; MJIB 2001, p. III; Ministry of Foreign Affairs 2018). Thereafter being one of the best ranked members that are subject to "regular follow-up", Chinese Taipei submitted biannual reports in 2021 and 2023 and is now preparing for the fourth round of mutual evaluations (AMLO 2024; Executive Yuan 2023).

Having learned valuable lessons from past peer reviews and national risk assessments (AMLO 2021), the government's current "ABC" strategy aims to *adapt* the legal framework, *block* fraudulent behavior and *cooperate* across borderlines (Executive Yuan 2024b). To equip law enforcement with modern tools, cardinal reforms were passed on 16 July 2024, introducing a Fraud Crime Hazard Prevention Act,[3] novel provisions for the deployment of science and technology in investigations,[4] as well as amendments to the Communication Security and Surveillance Act and the MLCA (Executive Yuan 2024a, c; Ministry of Justice 2024b) (see Fig. 5.1). For almost three decades, Taiwan's steadfast determination to stay in concordance with international standards has thus been a propelling force to push forward numerous ambitious agendas (Executive Yuan 2019).

[3] The original title in Chinese is 詐欺犯罪危害防制條例, available at the Laws & Regulations Database of the Republic of China (Taiwan) at https://law.moj.gov.tw/LawClass/LawAll.aspx?pcode=D0080226.

[4] The original title in Chinese is 科技偵查及保障法, available at the homepage of the Executive Yuan at https://www.ey.gov.tw/Page/24727DA92A709DBF/9b95e9b8-5d4d-4def-966c-80553239f706. In the wake of subsequent negotiations in the Legislative Yuan, the provisions were enacted not as an independent statute but incorporated into the Code of Criminal Procedure. See Sunrise Attorney-at-Law (2024).

Table 5.1 New definition of ML

Art. 3 **Directive 2018/1673 combating ML by criminal law**	**Art. 261** **German Criminal Code**	**Art. 2** **MLCA**
1. MS shall ensure following conduct is punishable as criminal conduct when committed intentionally	Wer einen Gegenstand der aus rechtswidrigen Tat herrührt Whoever, in respect of object derived from unlawful act	**本法所稱洗錢,指下列行為** the crime of ML is committed by any person who
(b) conceal/disguise true nature/source of property knowing property derived from criminal activity	1. **verbirgt** **hides**	**1. 隱匿 conceals** **掩飾 disguises**
(a) conversion/transfer of property knowing property derived from criminal activity for purpose of concealing/disguising illicit origin to **evade** legal **consequences**	2. in der Absicht **Ermittlung** zu **vereiteln** umtauscht/überträgt/verbringt exchanges/transfers/takes with intent of **preventing** it being **investigated**	**2. 妨礙或危害 調查/發現** **obstructs or jeopardizes** **investigation/discovery**
(c) possession/use of property knowing at time of receipt property was derived from criminal activity	3. **sich od. einem Dritten** verschafft procures for **themselves/third party** 4. **verwahrt** oder für **sich/Dritten verwendet** dessen Herkunft gekannt hat **uses** it for **themselves/third party** aware of its origin at time of obtaining **possession**	3. **持有/使用他人之犯罪所得** **possesses/uses** proceeds unlawful activity committed by **others** 4. **使用自己之犯罪所得** **use his/her** proceeds of unlawful activity

One of the preeminent goals of the 2024 reforms was to relax the definition for the offense of ML in Art. 2 MLCA to ease its compatibility with domestic criminal law (Legislative material 2024).[5] Interestingly, the German Criminal Code (German Federal Government 2020),[6] which implemented EU Directive 2018/1673 on "combating money laundering by criminal law"[7], served as a template (see Table 5.1). More generally, an analysis of the historic evolution of the MLCA highlights the role model effect of various laws, codifications and statutes from the EU (e.g. EU AMLDs, Directive 2014/42/EU on the freezing and confiscation of instrumentalities and proceeds of crime), European states (e.g. Germany, Austria, Ireland, Italy, Luxembourg, Netherlands, Spain, Switzerland, United Kingdom) and other countries (e.g. United States, Canada, Australia, Japan, Hongkong, Macao, South Korea), in addition to the importance of international references (e.g. UN Conventions, FATF Recommendations, APG evaluations) (Legislative material 2024). A perceptible assimilation with western concepts has thus generated a mixed synthesis that is not entirely—yet predominantly—in tune with the EU model.

5.2 Obliged Entities

A comparison of obliged entities in the EU and Taiwan exhibits following noteworthy differences: Art. 3 AML/CFT Regulation distinguishes between "credit institutions", "financial institutions" and "professional activities", whereas Art. 5 MLCA distinguishes between FIs and designated non-financial businesses and professions (DNFBPs). The list of FIs in Art. 5(1) MLCA covers 18 subcategories including banks, insurance companies, securities companies and "(o)ther financial institutions designated by the competent authorities in charge of the relevant industries." In other words, banks are subsumed under the heading "financial institutions" in Taiwan, whereas in the EU credit institutions are named as a separate category.

On the other hand, the EU subsumes CASPs under the heading "financial institutions", whereas enterprises or persons … providing virtual asset services are mentioned separately in Art. 5(2) MLCA but treated *on a par* with FIs.[8] The phrase "enterprises or persons … providing virtual *asset* services" was introduced to the MLCA in 2024 in line with FATF nomenclature of "virtual *asset* service providers (VASPs)" (Legislative material 2024; Ministry of Justice 2024a) and is almost identical with the EU's preferred terminology of "crypto-*asset* service providers"

[5] Criminal Code of the Republic of China, Art. 349 ("Offenses of Receiving Stolen Property").

[6] See (German Federal Ministry of Justice 2021) for an official version of the German Criminal Code, Section 261 ("Money laundering").

[7] Directive (EU) 2018/1673 of the European Parliament and of the Council of 23 October 2018 on combating money laundering by criminal law, OJ L 284, 12.11.2018, p. 22–30.

[8] Art. 5(2) MLCA.

(CASPs). It substitutes the older phrase "enterprises handling VC platforms or transactions",[9] which can easily be misunderstood as referring to currencies in a traditional sense.

Dating from a revision of the MLCA in November 2018, the scope of enterprises handling VC platforms or transactions was left to the discretion of the Executive Yuan.[10] Following a decree of the latter in April 2021 (Executive Yuan 2021a), the Financial Supervisory Commission (FSC) on 30 June 2021 announced an AML/CFT regulation wherein it defined the term VC and specified that respective enterprises engage in the business of safekeeping, administration or control of VCs, exchange VCs for fiat currencies (e.g. NT$, foreign currencies), exchange one and more forms of VCs, transfer VCs, and participate in and provide financial services related to the issuance or sale of VCs (Legislative material 2021).[11] Taking yet another leap towards closer alignment with the FATF, this regulation was amended and renamed in November 2024, notably by introducing the abbreviation VASP to define an "(e)nterprise or person providing virtual asset services that is registered and operates within the territory of Taiwan.[12] A related regulation concerning the AML registration of VASPs was published by the FSC on the same day, stating palpably that "(t)he scope of VASPs includes virtual asset exchanges providers, trading platforms, transferors, custodians, and underwriters".[13]

In retrospect, this era was ushered in with the Financial Technology Development and Innovative Experimentation Act (Experimentation Act)[14] promulgated in January 2018, which permitted eligible applicants to delve into unconventional fintech projects under privileged circumstances during the trial period.[15] Manifestly supporting flexible adaptations to unprecedented phenomena, the law left no doubt that recognized AML/CFT safeguards must not be compromised.[16] The Financial Supervisory Commission (FSC) as the designated competent authority prescribed

[9] Art. 5(2) MLCA, as promulgated on 7 Nov. 2018.

[10] Art. 5(4) MLCA, as promulgated on 7 Nov. 2018.

[11] Art. 2 Regulations Governing AML/CFT for Enterprises Handling VC Platform or Transaction (VC Regulations) 虛擬通貨平台及交易業務事業防制洗錢及打擊資恐辦法.

[12] Art. 2 Regulations Governing AML/CFT for Enterprises or Persons Providing Virtual Asset Services (VA Regulations) 提供虛擬資產服務之事業或人員防制洗錢及打擊資恐辦法.

[13] Art. 2 Regulations Governing AML Registration of Enterprises or Persons Providing Virtual Asset Services (VASP Registration Regulations) 提供虛擬資產服務之事業或人員洗錢防制登記辦法.

[14] The original title in Chinese is 金融科技發展與創新實驗條例, available at the Laws & Regulations Database of the Republic of China (Taiwan) at https://law.moj.gov.tw/LawClass/LawAll.aspx?pcode=G0380254.

[15] Art. 26 Experimentation Act.

[16] According to Art. 25 Experimentation Act "the provisions of the Money Laundering Control Act, Terrorism Financing Suppression Act and related regulations, orders or administrative rules will still apply".

respective details in the 2019 Regulations Governing AML/CTF of Financial Technology Innovative Experimentation (Experimentation Regulations),[17] reiterating that traditional FIs[18] are bound by AML/CFT provisions in pertinent laws and regulations when experimenting with financial technologies.[19]

Unlike the highly developed financial sector, the category of DNFBPs in Art. 5(3) MLCA initially only constrained dealers in precious metals and stones (APG 2019, p. 270). In the meantime, it has made great strides and henceforth covers six subcategories: Jewelry businesses; land administration agents and real estate agencies; lawyers, notaries and accountants; trust and company services providers. "Enterprises or persons that provide third-party payment services"[20] have been classified as DNFBPs by the Executive Yuan since August 2021 (Executive Yuan 2021b) based on the general catch all clause "(o)ther enterprises or persons, with the characteristics of their operation or transaction modes likely involved in money laundering"[21] but are—as of 2024—expressly mentioned in the MLCA (Legislative material 2024).

Latest amendments enjoin service providers of virtual assets and third-party payments from providing services in Taiwan unless they have completed formal registration procedures.[22] Hereby honoring FATF Recommendation 15 ("New technologies") and Recommendation 28 ("Regulation and supervision of DNFBPs") (Legislative material 2024) is something that was not accomplished abruptly, but has been evolving over years (Administration for Digital Industries 2023; FSC 2021). As a matter of fact, the mode how enterprises or persons providing virtual asset services and third-party payment services slowly matured into fully-fledged obliged entities portrays a legal culture that favors flexible administrative guidance based

[17] The original title in Chinese is 金融科技創新實驗防制洗錢及打擊資恐辦法, available at the Laws & Regulations Database of the Republic of China (Taiwan) at https://law.moj.gov.tw/LawClass/LawAll.aspx?pcode=G0380266.

[18] Defined in Art. 2 of the Regulations Governing AML of FIs 金融機構防制洗錢辦法 (FIs Regulations).

[19] Art. 1 Experimentation Regulations.

[20] Third party payment service providers are defined in Art. 2 Regulations Governing AML/CFT for Enterprises or Persons Providing Third-Party Payment Services (Third-Party Payment Regulations) 提供第三方支付服務之事業或人員防制洗錢及打擊資恐辦法 as "a business that is not an electronic payment institution, as defined in the Act Governing Electronic Payment Institutions, and which provides the service of collecting and making payments for online real transactions as an agent."

[21] Art. 5(3) MLCA.

[22] Art. 6 MLCA. On this basis, the FSC promulgated the VASP Registration Regulations in November 2024 after deliberating the IOSCO "Considerations Relating to Crypto-Asset Trading Platforms" (2020) and "Recommendations for Crypto and Digital Asset Markets" (2023), the FATF Interpretive Notes to Recommendation 15 and its "Updated Guidance for a Risk-Based Approach to Virtual Assets and Virtual Asset Service Providers" (2021), the EU MiCA Regulation, the UK's "Money Laundering, Terrorist Financing and Transfer of Funds (Information on the Payer) Regulations 2017" and other laws, regulations and guidelines from Japan, Korea, Hongkong and Taiwan; cf. FSC (2025).

Table 5.2 Comparison of obliged entities in the EU and Taiwan

AML/CFT REGULATION	MLCA
CREDIT INSTITUTIONS AND FINANCIAL INSTITUTIONS (FIs)	
distinction between credit institutions and FIs	FIs incl. banks other FIs designated by competent authorities
FIs incl. CASPs	provisions governing FIs shall apply to VASPs
NATURAL/LEGAL PERSONS EXERCISING PROFESSIONAL ACTIVITIES	**DNFBP** **非金融事業或人員**
traders in precious metals/stones + cultural /high-value goods	jewelry business **銀樓業**
estate agents in real estate transactions incl. letting immovable property monthly rent EUR 10,000	land administration agents and **real estate agencies** transactions concerning purchase/sale of real estate
lawyers, notaries, accountants **律師、公證人、會計師**	
trust and company service providers **信託及公司服務提供業**	
	third party payment service providers **提供第三方支付服務之事業或員**
credit intermediaries for mortgage and consumer credits non-financial mixed activity holding companies crowdfunding service providers / intermediaries investment migration operators football agents, professional football clubs	other businesses or professions likely involved in ML **其他業務特性或交易型態易為洗錢犯罪利用之事業或從業人員**
providers of gambling services	illegal (Criminal Code, Chapter 21)
reliance on third parties	
outsourcing	

on mutual consensus and gradual transitions *in lieu of* confrontational rigid maneuvers or sudden changes of blackletter law (APG 2019, p. 42; Wang and Chiu 2014, pp. 8–9; Liang et al. 2023).

Other incipient players introduced by the EU in 2024 (especially service providers in the fields of crowdfunding, investment migration, sports, professional traders in cultural goods and high-value goods) are not *per se* mentioned in Taiwanese law, but might still be encapsulated in Art. 5 MLCA due to its non-exhaustive enumeration of obliged entities. In view of the government's commitment to a liberal business climate while upholding financial integrity and security, it can be anticipated that the list of obliged entities will be adjusted in due time, if necessary. As far as reliance on third parties is concerned, doing so in the context of CDD is prohibited for notaries,[23] but otherwise permitted for attorneys[24] and—under certain conditions—also possible for agricultural financial institutions,[25] certified public accountants,[26] financial leasing enterprises,[27] and VASPs[28] (see Table 5.2).

5.3 Customer Due Diligence

Following the maxim of compulsory CDD stipulated in Art. 8 MLCA, obliged entities must verify the identity of customers and BOs, wherefore obliged entities must not accept anonymous accounts or accounts in fictitious names in their business relationships. Among others,[29] this was spelled out by the FSC for FIs in 2017[30] and for enterprises handling VC platforms or transactions in 2021.[31] In the same spirit, the travel rule applies to domestic wire transfers,[32] cross-border wire transfers[33] and VA transfers alike. As a corollary, where a VASP serves as the originating party of VA transfers, it shall obtain information regarding the customer transferring the VAs

[23] Art. 9 Regulations Governing AML/CFT for Notaries (Notaries Regulations) 公證人防制洗錢及打擊資恐辦法.

[24] Art. 6-1 Regulations on AML/CFT Operations Matters Conducted by Attorneys (Attorneys Regulations) 律師辦理防制洗錢及打擊資恐作業辦法.

[25] Art. 7 Regulations Governing AML of Agricultural FIs (Agricultural FIs Regulations) 農業金融機構防制洗錢辦法.

[26] Art. 11 Regulations Governing AML/CFT for Certified Public Accountants (Accountants Regulations) 會計師防制洗錢及打擊資恐辦法.

[27] Art. 7 Regulations Governing AML of Financial Leasing Enterprises (Leasing Enterprises Regulations) 辦理融資性租賃業務事業防制洗錢辦法.

[28] Art. 3 VA Regulations.

[29] See e.g. Art. 3 Agricultural FIs Regulations; Art. 7 Accountants Regulations; Art. 3 Leasing Enterprises Regulations.

[30] Art. 3 FIs Regulations.

[31] Art. 3 VC Regulations.

[32] See e.g. Art. 5 Regulations Governing Internal Audit and Internal Control System of AML/CT of Agricultural FIs 防制洗錢與打擊資恐內部控制及稽核制度實施辦法, requiring agricultural FIs to provide information on the originator and beneficiary accompanying the wire transfer.

[33] Art. 8 Experimentation Regulations requires applicants to provide "accurate information on the originator and beneficiary accompanying the wire transfer".

(originator) and the customer receiving the VAs (beneficiary), and submit this information to the enterprise serving as the beneficiary party.[34] For this provision to be fully realized, an effective date must be specified by the FSC,[35] which has been postponed until implementation of the travel rule is widely recognized by international counterparts (Chang and Attorneys 2021). On 26 Sept. 2023, the FSC published its VASP guiding principles, indicating that implementation will be incremental like in Japan and initially focus on transactions exceeding certain thresholds (FSC 2023, pp. 14–15; 2025).

Cash transactions and transactions using electronic stored value cards above the amount of NT$500,000 are normally subject to additional requisites (e.g. reporting) (APG 2019, p. 54).[36] For payments that exceed certain thresholds, the Ministry of Justice may in consultation with central competent authorities prescribe non-cash payment tools.[37] In other words, making large cash payments anonymously can be utterly proscribed. For the same reasons, companies may since 2018 no longer issue bearer shares (APG 2019, p. 185).[38] As to those bearer shares that have already been issued, customers must be urged to update the beneficial ownership information.[39] Apart from anonymous products, certain relationships (e.g. correspondent relationships with shell institutions) are forbidden *ab initio* (APG 2019, p. 256)[40] (see Table 5.3).

Vis-à-vis high-risk countries or regions, competent authorities may request FIs and DNFBPs to strengthen "measures for verification of customer's identity during transactions", to "limit or prohibit" such transfers and to undertake "other necessary preventive measures".[41] Enhanced CDD shall also be applied when confronted with PEPs, their family members and close associates.[42] A look at the details fleshed out by the Ministry of Justice surprises with a long slate of PEPs, including domestic directors and speakers of "municipal, county and city governments"[43] and foreign "senior executives of state owned corporations".[44] Close associates are defined as

---

[34] Art. 7 VA Regulations.

[35] Art. 18 VA Regulations.

[36] See e.g. Art. 2 FIs Regulations; Art. 11 VA Regulations, setting a threshold of NT$500,000; Art. 16 The Act Governing Electronic Payment Institutions 電子支付機構管理條例.

[37] Art. 5(5) MLCA.

[38] According to Art. 162 Company Act "(a) registered share certificate shall bear the true name of the shareholder".

[39] Art. 7 Accountants Regulations; Art. 3 FIs Regulations; Art. 3 Agricultural FIs Regulations; Art. 3 Leasing Enterprises Regulations; Art. 3 VA Regulations.

[40] Art. 3 Regulations Governing Internal Audit and Internal Control System of AML/CFT of Banking Business and Other FIs Designated by the FSC 銀行業及其他經金融監督管理委員會指定之金融機構防制洗錢及打擊資恐內部控制與稽核制度實施辦法.

[41] Art. 9 MLCA.

[42] Art. 8 MLCA.

[43] Art. 2(12) and (13) Standards for Determining the Scope of Politically Exposed Persons Entrusted with Prominent Public Function, Their Family Members and Close Associates (PEPs Standards) 重要政治性職務之人與其家庭成員及有密切關係之人範圍認定標準.

[44] Art. 3 PEPs Standards.

Table 5.3 Prohibition of anonymous transactions in the EU and in Taiwan

<table>
<tr><th>EU</th><th>TAIWAN</th></tr>
<tr><td colspan="2">no anonymous accounts (incl. VAs)</td></tr>
<tr><td colspan="2">travel rule applies to transfer of funds / VAs</td></tr>
<tr><td colspan="2">cash restrictions</td></tr>
<tr><td colspan="2">prepaid cards / electronic stored value cards that exceed certain amount</td></tr>
<tr><td colspan="2">companies shall no longer issue bearer shares</td></tr>
<tr><td colspan="2">correspondent relationships with shell institutions</td></tr>
</table>

persons with a "close social or professional relationship", such as partners, "senior executives of the same corporation", or employees[45] (see Table 5.4). The fact that the APG rated Taiwan in this category as noncompliant back in 2007 and compliant with FATF standards in 2019 (APG 2019, pp. 254–255) evidences Taiwan's perseverance and resolve to excel.

Attesting general compliance with FATF Recommendation 10 ("Customer due diligence") and Recommendation 22 ("DNFBPs: Customer due diligence"), the APG in 2019 advised additional guidance for DNFBPs offering company and trust services (APG 2019, pp. 179–190). Indeed, lawyers as well as trust and company service providers dealing with legal entities or arrangements must be vigilant when conducting CDD. A comparison of these two categories of DNFBPs shows that their status as obliged entities in Taiwan and in the EU is mostly congruent, if not identical (see Tables 5.5 and 5.6).

The scope, procedure and method of CDD is specified in administrative regulations of central competent authorities in charge of the relevant industries. A systematic collection covering FIs and DNFBPs that is available at the homepage of the Ministry of Justice Investigation Bureau (2017b) markedly refers to regulations for

[45] Art. 7 PEPs Standards.

Table 5.4 Enhanced CDD in the EU and in Taiwan

<table>
<tr><th>EU</th><th>TAIWAN</th></tr>
<tr><td colspan="2">high risk third countries</td></tr>
<tr><td colspan="2">politically exposed persons
international, national, regional, local level
senior executives in government-controlled enterprises
family members
close associates</td></tr>
</table>

Table 5.5 Legal professionals

<table>
<tr><th>EU AML/CFT Regulation
Art. 3(3)(a) and (b)</th><th>MLCA
Art. 5(3)(3)</th></tr>
<tr><td>auditors, external accountants, tax advisors</td><td>accountants
會計師</td></tr>
<tr><td colspan="2">notaries, lawyers planning/carrying out following transactions for client
律師、公證人為客戶準備或進行下列交易時</td></tr>
<tr><td colspan="2">1.
buy/sell real property, business entities
買賣不動產, 事業體</td></tr>
<tr><td colspan="2">2.
manage client money, securities, other assets incl. crypto
管理客戶金錢、證券或其他資產</td></tr>
<tr><td colspan="2">3.
manage accounts (bank, savings, securities, crypto)
管理銀行、儲蓄或證券帳戶</td></tr>
<tr><td colspan="2">4.
organize contributions for creation/operation/management of companies
有關提供公司設立、營運或管理之資金籌劃</td></tr>
<tr><td colspan="2">5.
creation/operation/management of
設立/營運/管理</td></tr>
<tr><td>trusts, companies, foundations, similar structures</td><td>legal persons/agreements
法人或法律協議</td></tr>
</table>

Table 5.6 Trust and company service providers

<table>
<tr><th>EU AML/CFT Regulation
Art. 2(1)(11), 3(3)(c)</th><th>MLCA
Art. 5(3)(4)</th></tr>
<tr><td>trust or company service providers

natural/legal person that by way of its business provides any of following services to third parties:</td><td>trust and company service providers

when they prepare for or carry out transactions for client concerning following transactions:</td></tr>
<tr><td colspan="2">1.
formation of legal person</td></tr>
<tr><td colspan="2">2.
acting as or arranging for another person to act as director/secretary of company, partner of partnership, similar position in other legal persons</td></tr>
<tr><td colspan="2">3.
providing registered office, business address, correspondence/administrative address, other related services for company, partnership or other legal person or legal arrangement</td></tr>
<tr><td colspan="2">4.
acting as, or arranging for another person to act as trustee of a trust performing equivalent function for another/similar legal arrangement</td></tr>
<tr><td colspan="2">5.
acting as, or arranging for another person to act as a nominee shareholder for another person</td></tr>
</table>

attorneys,[46] notaries[47] and accountants.[48] For trust and company service providers, a bespoke regulation has not been enacted. Yet falling within the scope of a recent regulation directed at trustees of non-trust enterprises, they too will have to proactively inform competent authorities and business partners about true identities in accordance with specifications of the Ministry of Justice.[49] More on this in the next section.

5.4 Beneficial Ownership

The most formidable challenge is the discernment of beneficial ownership. Somewhat compounding the problem, Art. 8 MLCA equates customers with BOs but does not clarify its meaning. Instead, it is the "central competent authority in charge of the

[46] Art. 3-9 Attorneys Regulations.

[47] Art. 9–18 Notaries Regulations.

[48] Art. 7 Accountants Regulations.

[49] Art. 11 MLCA; Measures for Filing, Updating and Reporting of Trustee Information and Disclosure of Trust Status for Non-trust Sectors under Article 11, Paragraph 6 of the Money Laundering Control Act (Measures for Non-trust Sectors) 洗錢防制法第十一條第六項非信託業之受託人資訊申報更新申報及信託地位揭露辦法 promulgated in November 2024. See Ministry of Justice 2024c, with references to the FATF's "Guidance for a Risk-Based Approach for Trust and Company Service Providers" (2019), "Guidance on Beneficial Ownership of Legal Persons" (2023), "Guidance on Beneficial Ownership and Transparency of Legal Arrangements" (2024).

relevant industries … in consultation with the Ministry of Justice and other related government agencies" who shall regulate the scope, procedures and methods of CDD.[50] As a result, a plethora of administrative regulations explicate the term BO with some slight alterations, usually referring to a natural person who ultimately owns or controls a customer or on whose behalf a transaction is being conducted.[51]

Differentiated ways for identifying BOs of legal persons or organizations allude to a controlling ownership interest of more than 25% of the shares, control through other means and senior managing officials.[52] In the event of trusts or similar legal agreements, an understanding of the control structure shall be gained, among others by identifying persons in certain positions or belonging to certain classes (e.g. settlor, trustee, director, manager, supervisor, administrator, beneficiary) and requesting documents from the customer which prove the owner or BO.[53] Foundations are governed by a Foundations Act[54] and a respective regulation, which requires due diligence investigations on beneficiaries for purposes of risk assessment, albeit without specifying how to identify BOs[55] (see Table 5.7).

Inserting a uniform taxonomy in the MLCA itself could fill the gaps, curb dispensable repetitions and foster a streamlined regulatory environment, whilst leaving room for requisite variations. To satisfy EU standards, it is moreover imperative that legal entities, BOs, trustees and persons holding equivalent positions in similar legal arrangements themselves be pressured to reveal their status and furnish adequate, accurate and up-to-date BO information. Hitherto, the burden of verifying the identity of BOs has been overwhelmingly placed on FIs and DNFBPs, who routinely rely on data retrieval systems, formal checklists and self-declarations. Conversely, legal persons and trustees have in the past rarely been coerced amid minimal disclosure requirements (APG 2019, pp. 135–144, 179–190, 283–289, 338–339).

Some of these omission were rectified in 2018 by amending the Company Act[56]: Bringing to attention influential insiders who might not conspicuously hold a leading position within a company, liability was allocated to a "responsible person" who *de facto* has control over "the management of the personnel, financial or business operation of the company and *de facto* instructs a director to conduct business".[57] What is more, a company shall report "its directors, supervisors, managerial officers,

---

[50] Art. 8(4) MLCA.

[51] See e.g. Art. 2 Agricultural FIs Regulations; Art. 2 Accountants Regulations; Art. 2 FIs Regulations; Art. 2 Regulations Governing AML/CTF for Land Administration Agents and Real Estate Brokerages (Brokerages Regulations) 地政士及不動產經紀業防制洗錢及打擊資恐辦法; Art. 2 Leasing Enterprises Regulations; Art. 2 Experimentation Regulations; Art. 2 VA Regulations.

[52] See e.g. Art. 3 Agricultural FIs Regulations; Art. 7 Accountants Regulations; Art. 3 FIs Regulations; Art. 3 Leasing Enterprises Regulations; Art. 3 VA Regulations.

[53] Art. 6 Attorneys Regulations; Art. 10–11 Notaries Regulations.

[54] Foundations Act 財團法人法 (2018).

[55] Art. 4 Regulations on Competent Authorities Governing Specific Foundations for AML/CTF 主管機關辦理特定財團法人洗錢及資恐防制辦法.

[56] The original title in Chinese is 公司法, available at the Laws & Regulations Database of the Republic of China (Taiwan) at https://law.moj.gov.tw/LawClass/LawAll.aspx?pcode=J0080001.

[57] Art. 8 Company Act.

Table 5.7 Beneficial ownership definitions in the EU and Taiwan

<table>
<tr><th>EU</th><th>TAIWAN</th></tr>
<tr><td colspan="2">BO
NATURAL PERSON

who ultimately
OWNS
25%

or

CONTROLS
a customer via other means

or
on whose behalf a transaction is being conducted

persons in certain positions
settlors, trustees
directors, managers
supervisors, administrators
beneficiaries</td></tr>
</table>

and shareholders holding more than 10 percent of the total shares … by way of electronic transmission" or else face serious consequences (including nullification of its incorporation registration).[58] For this reason, nominee directors and nominee shareholders should be registered once they hold more than 10% of a company's capital or shares (APG 2019, pp. 183–187).[59] Endowed with abundant powers (e.g. to request assistance from other authorities, civil institutions or groups), the Ministry of Economic Affairs (MOEA) as the central competent authority shall "regularly verify the accuracy, timeliness and completeness" of the information accessible at the Company Transparency Platform (https://ctp.tdcc.com.tw), which therefore is a valuable source of reference for government authorities, FIs and DNFBPs.[60]

[58] Art. 22-1 Company Act.

[59] Whereas the Company Act does not expressly define nominee shareholders, Art. 5 MLCA notes that DNFBPs include trust and company service providers who act as or arrange "for another person to act as a nominee shareholder", albeit without specifying the term nominee shareholder.

[60] Art. 11, 15, 16 Regulations Governing Reporting and Management of Information on Article 22 Bis of the Company Act 公司法第二十二條之一資料申報及管理辦法.

Big breakthroughs were at last achieved in 2024 by revamping the MLCA: Bearing in mind FATF Recommendation 25 ("Transparency and beneficial ownership of legal arrangements") and UK Regulation 2017 No. 692 (Legislative material 2024; Ministry of Justice 2024a),[61] Art. 11 MLCA was newly formulated, whereby trustees of non-trust enterprises must obtain, declare and update certain information (about settlors, trustees, beneficiaries, other natural persons exercising ultimate effective control, agents, service providers) and proactively disclose their position when forming business relationships with FIs or DNFBPs or conducting occasional transactions that reach certain thresholds. Details substantiated by the Ministry of Justice do not distinguish between domestic and foreign legal arrangements but generally refer to single or cumulative transactions reaching NT$500,00 or the equivalent value in foreign currencies.[62] Another shortcoming is the rampant abuse of fake identities in the financial sector, namely by making available, collecting and using personal account information without justifiable reasons or via improper means. To enjoin these popular tactics of circumventing CDD, the sphere of Art. 20–22 MLCA has been extended to cover FIs, VASPs and third-party payment providers alike (Ministry of Justice 2024a, p. 24).

Stepping up public-private collaboration, the Fraud Crime Hazard Prevention Act passed in 2024 finally describes FIs and VASPs as "good administrator(s)" who must exercise due care and "cooperate with the judiciary police department to form a joint defense reporting system",[63] rather than simply refusing or declining a business relationship or transaction when a customer is suspected of using a nominee.[64] This will surely sharpen the ability of law enforcement to intervene (Silva 2019, p. 66), while tracing hidden BOs behind layers of shell companies and middlemen (AMLO 2021).

---

[61] Ministry of Justice (2024a, pp. 14–16) with references to the UK's Money Laundering, Terrorist Financing and Transfer of Funds (Information on the Payer) Regulations 2017.

[62] Art. 5 Measures for Non-trust Sectors. Cf. in this context the EU's rigorous stance that legal entities and legal arrangements from abroad must file their beneficial ownership information in a central register as a precondition for valid business relationships, high value acquisitions, and public procurement contracts in the EU; see AML/CFT Regulation, Rec. 55, 132, 133, Art. 2(1)(19), 67; 6th AMLD, Rec. 44.

[63] Art. 8, 10 Fraud Crime Hazard Prevention Act.

[64] Art. 4 Regulations Governing AML/CFT for Jewelry Businesses 銀樓業防制洗錢與打擊資恐辦法; Art. 4 Agricultural FIs Regulations; Art. 8 Accountants Regulations; Art. 9 Brokerages Regulations; Art. 4 FIs Regulations; Art. 15 Notaries Regulations; Art. 4 Experimentation Regulations; Art. 4 VA Regulations; Art. 8 Third-Party Payment Regulations.

5.5 Sanctions

A variety of administrative, civil and criminal sanctions, including imprisonment, court orders (e.g. prohibiting withdrawals, transfers, payments, deliveries or assignments, other necessary dispositions of property),[65] confiscations (e.g. cash, property),[66] fines, and other preventive and punitive measures loom over anyone found to be in transgression. Nonetheless, the APG in its third round of evaluation deplored that penalties were not proportionate or dissuasive (APG 2019, pp. 87–88, 315–317).

Mindful of this criticism, the 2024 reforms contemplate aggravated sanctions that can be inflicted recurrently each time an offense occurs, lifting the upper ceilings to NT$100 million for monetary fines and a maximum of 10 years imprisonment.[67] Irrespective of any fixed amounts, obliged entities that do not adhere to statutory cash limits can be fined twice the amount of illegal transactions.[68] In analogy to existing domestic laws (e.g. Act Governing Food Safety and Sanitation,[69] Water Pollution Control Act,[70] Air Pollution Control Act[71]) (Legislative material 2024), legal entities can even be fined ten times more than natural persons when bearing imputed liability for their representatives, agents, and employees.[72] Besides, the withdrawal of authorizations (notably revocation or suspension of license or registration for VASPs) is now anchored in the MLCA.[73] In synergy with other reform measures, competent authorities are thus bestowed with an enriched AML/CFT toolbox that promises to have more deterrent effect (see Table 5.8).

[65] Art. 18 MLCA.

[66] Art. 14, 25 MLCA.

[67] Art. 19 MLCA; Ministry of Justice (2024a, pp. 6–27).

[68] Art. 5 MLCA.

[69] The original title in Chinese is 食品安全衛生管理法, available at the Laws & Regulations Database of the Republic of China (Taiwan) at https://law.moj.gov.tw/LawClass/LawAll.aspx?pcode=L0040001.

[70] The original title in Chinese is 水污染防治法, available at the Laws & Regulations Database of the Republic of China (Taiwan) at https://law.moj.gov.tw/LawClass/LawAll.aspx?pcode=O0040001.

[71] The original title in Chinese is 空氣污染防制法, available at the Laws & Regulations Database of the Republic of China (Taiwan) at https://law.moj.gov.tw/LawClass/LawAll.aspx?pcode=O0020001.

[72] Art. 6, 23 MLCA.

[73] Art. 6 MLCA. See also Art. 22-1 Company Act according to which a company's incorporation registration may be nullified when it refuses to report directors, supervisors, managerial officers, and shareholders holding more than 10% of the total shares.

Table 5.8 Comparison of sanctions in the EU and Taiwan

EU	TAIWAN
criminal sanctions	
MS	10y imprisonment, NT$ 100 million
administrative measures incl. withdrawal/suspension of authorizations	
periodic pecuniary sanctions	
max. 3% daily turnover (legal person) max. 2 % daily income (natural person)	**no upper limit** specified in MLCA possible
pecuniary sanctions against credit and FI	
max. EUR 10 million / 10% annual turnover (legal person) max. EUR 5 million (natural person)	max. NT$ 10 million (FI) max. NT$ 5 million (DNFBPs)
pecuniary sanctions	
max. 2 x benefit EUR 1 million (serious/repeated/systematic breaches)	2 x transaction amount (noncompliance with cash limits)
imputed liability of legal entities	
	10 x more than natural person

References

Administration for Digital Industries (2023, July 28) 第三方支付法規專區. https://moda.gov.tw/ADI/services/laws&regulations/related-law-and-regulation-of-adi/5747. Accessed 2 Dec 2024

Anti-Money Laundering Office (AMLO), Executive Yuan (2017, updated 2024, September 4) Overview. https://www.amlo.moj.gov.tw/1523/1524/1525/4093/post. Affairs, https://www.amlo.moj.gov.tw/1523/1524/1526/4097/post

Anti-Money Laundering Office (AMLO), Executive Yuan (2018, May) National Money Laundering and Terrorist Financing Risk Assessment Report. https://www.fsc.gov.tw/fckdowndoc?file=/National%20Risk%20Assessment%20Report.pdf&flag=doc

Anti-Money Laundering Office (AMLO), Executive Yuan (2021) National Money Laundering, Terrorist Financing and Proliferation Financing Risk Assessment Report. https://www.amlo.moj.gov.tw/media/20214028/2021-national-money-laundering-terrorist-financing-and-proliferation-financing-risk-assessment-report_en.pdf?mediaDL=true

Anti-Money Laundering Office (AMLO), Executive Yuan (2024, September 4) Taiwan maintains excellent ratings on money laundering prevention [News]. https://www.amlo.moj.gov.tw/1523/1524/1528/42811

Asia/Pacific Group on Money Laundering (APG) (2007, July 24) APG Mutual Evaluation Report on Chinese Taipei. https://apgml.org/members-and-observers/members/member-documents.aspx?m=28699d47-c110-43cf-883a-e359c2081828
Asia/Pacific Group on Money Laundering (APG) (2019, October) Anti-money laundering and counter-terrorist financing measures – Chinese Taipei, Third Round Mutual Evaluation Report. https://apgml.org/members-and-observers/members/member-documents.aspx?m=28699d47-c110-43cf-883a-e359c2081828. https://www.fatf-gafi.org/media/fatf/documents/reports/mer-fsrb/APG-Mutual-Evaluation-Report-Chinese-Taipei%20-%20October%202019.pdf
Asia/Pacific Group on Money Laundering (APG) (2024) Chinese Taipei. https://apgml.org/members-and-observers/members/details.aspx?m=28699d47-c110-43cf-883a-e359c2081828. Accessed 2 Dec 2024
Chang A, Xiri Attorneys (2021, July 15) Taiwan's Money Laundering Control Act Applies To Virtual Currency Businesses. https://www.mondaq.com/money-laundering/1091650/taiwan39s-money-laundering-control-act-applies-to-virtual-currency-businesses
Egmont Group (2024) EG Member FIU Information. https://egmontgroup.org/members-by-region/eg-member-fiu-information/. Accessed 2 Dec 2024
Executive Yuan (2019, November 21) Third-round APG mutual evaluation. https://english.ey.gov.tw/News3/9E5540D592A5FECD/6fd57fe8-dc6e-4519-a572-9bf0632fa9ef
Executive Yuan (2021a, April 7) Decree no. 1100167722. https://www.mjib.gov.tw/userfiles/files/35-%E6%B4%97%E9%8C%A2%E9%98%B2%E5%88%B6%E8%99%95/files/%E6%8E%88%E6%AC%8A%E5%91%BD%E4%BB%A4/02-05-85.pdf
Executive Yuan (2021b, August 18) Decree no. 1100181600. https://www.mjib.gov.tw/userfiles/files/35-%E6%B4%97%E9%8C%A2%E9%98%B2%E5%88%B6%E8%99%95/files/%E6%8E%88%E6%AC%8A%E5%91%BD%E4%BB%A4/02-05-87.pdf
Executive Yuan (2023, November 28) 我國提交追蹤報告再獲 APG 肯定 持續維持亞太最佳成績 [Press Releases]. https://www.ey.gov.tw/Page/9277F759E41CCD91/65e31fb1-8a19-4334-b46b-e720c0ff3fe2
Executive Yuan (2024a, May 9) Cabinet approves four draft bills to bolster anti-fraud capabilities [Press Releases]. https://english.ey.gov.tw/Page/61BF20C3E89B856/075117fd-6122-4f0e-bb38-a658306d6c59
Executive Yuan (2024b, October 21) 出席APG評鑑員訓練研討會開幕 卓揆:臺灣與各國政府共同負起打擊犯罪責任 守護世界安全穩定 [Press Releases]. https://www.ey.gov.tw/Page/9277F759E41CCD91/c1a63a5f-6f20-41e2-bed2-3ccd44d1fddb
Executive Yuan (2024c, November 28) Updated anti-fraud strategy introduces stronger protections [Press Releases]. https://english.ey.gov.tw/Page/61BF20C3E89B856/60819cf0-b10f-4b99-bb25-12f82583a26a
Financial Supervisory Commission (FSC), Republic of China (Taiwan) (2021, March 19) 洗錢防制與打擊資恐專區. https://www.fsc.gov.tw/ch/home.jsp?id=849&parentpath=0,2,310
Financial Supervisory Commission (FSC), Republic of China (Taiwan) (2023, September 26) 金融監督管理委員會管理虛擬資產平台及交易業務事業 (VASP) 指導原則. https://www.fsc.gov.tw/userfiles/file/%E9%87%91%E8%9E%8D%E7%9B%A3%E7%9D%A3%E7%AE%A1%E7%90%86%E5%A7%94%E5%93%A1%E6%9C%83%E7%AE%A1%E7%90%86%E8%99%9B%E6%93%AC%E8%B3%87%E7%94%A2%E5%B9%B3%E5%8F%B0%E5%8F%8A%E4%BA%A4%E6%98%93%E6%A5%AD%E5%8B%99%E4%BA%8B%E6%A5%AD%EF%BC%88VASP%EF%BC%89%E6%8C%87%E5%B0%8E%E5%8E%9F%E5%89%87(1).pdf
Financial Supervisory Commission (FSC), Republic of China (Taiwan) (2025, May 13) 提供虛擬資產服務之事業或人員. https://www.sfb.gov.tw/ch/home.jsp?id=1053&parentpath=0%2C8

German Federal Government (Bundesregierung) (2020) Entwurf eines Gesetzes zur Verbesserung der strafrechtlichen Bekämpfung der Geldwäsche. https://www.bundesrat.de/SharedDocs/drucksachen/2020/0601-0700/620-20.pdf?__blob=publicationFile&v=1. Accessed 2 Dec 2024
German Federal Ministry of Justice (2021) German Criminal Code. https://www.bgbl.de/xaver/bgbl/start.xav#__bgbl__%2F%2F*%5B%40attr_id%3D%27bgbl121s0327.pdf%27%5D__1723778687010. Accessed 2 Dec 2024
Lee LLC (1996) Combating illicit narcotics traffic in Taiwan: the proposed money laundering control act. Tulane J Int Comparative Law 4(2):189–244
Legislative material (2021, June 30) 虛擬通貨平台及交易業務事業防制洗錢及打擊資恐辦法總說明(110.06.30 訂定). Ministry of Justice, Database of the Republic of China (Taiwan). https://law.moj.gov.tw/LawClass/LawHistory.aspx?pcode=G0380268. Accessed 2 Dec 2024
Legislative material (2024, July 16) 洗錢防制法. Ministry of Justice, Database of the Republic of China (Taiwan). https://law.moj.gov.tw/LawClass/LawAll.aspx?pcode=G0380131. Accessed 2 Dec 2024
Legislative Yuan (2024) 重要通過法案. 修正洗錢防制法. https://www.ly.gov.tw/Pages/Detail.aspx?nodeid=33324&pid=242196. Accessed 2 Dec 2024
Liang S-H, Lin H-C, Hsiao H-Y (2023) Compliance and governance: evidence from financial institutions in Taiwan. J Financ Regul Compliance 31(3):298–315. https://doi.org/10.1108/JFRC-03-2022-0038
Ministry of Foreign Affairs, Republic of China (Taiwan) (2018, May 3) 1st national report on money laundering released in Taiwan. Taiwan Today. https://taiwanreview.nat.gov.tw/news.php?unit=10&post=133671&unitname=Society-Top-News&postname=1st-national-report-on-money-laundering-released-in-Taiwan
Ministry of Justice (2024a, July 16) 洗錢防制法修正草案條文對照表. https://www.ljc.moj.gov.tw/media/367232/1130716_%E6%B4%97%E9%98%B2%E6%B3%95%E5%85%A8%E6%96%87%E4%BF%AE%E6%AD%A3%E5%B0%8D%E7%85%A7%E8%A1%A8%E4%B8%89%E8%AE%80%E6%A2%9D%E6%96%87.pdf?mediaDL=true. Accessed 2 Dec 2024
Ministry of Justice (2024b, September 18) 打詐新四法專區. https://www.moj.gov.tw/2204/2645/181663/181665/218067/post
Ministry of Justice (2024c, November 25) Explanations to "Measures for Filing, Updating and Reporting of Trustee Information and Disclosure of Trust Status for Non-trust Sectors under Article 11, Paragraph 6 of the Money Laundering Control Act" 洗錢防制法第十一條第六項非信託業之受託人資訊申報更新申報及信託地位揭露辦法. https://law.moj.gov.tw/LawClass/LawGetFile.ashx?FileId=0000379657&lan=C&type=1&date=20241125
Ministry of Justice Investigation Bureau (MJIB) (2001) Anti-Money Laundering Annual Report, 2001. https://www.mjib.gov.tw/EditPage/?PageID=46098253-f0e9-46e4-9832-b96e17e00c71; https://www.mjib.gov.tw/userfiles/files/35-%E6%B4%97%E9%8C%A2%E9%98%B2%E5%88%B6%E8%99%95/files/%E6%B4%97%E9%8C%A2%E9%98%B2%E5%88%B6%E8%99%95-EN/2001yearbook.pdf
Ministry of Justice Investigation Bureau (MJIB) (2017a, August 3; updated 2019, November 13) Overview of the Anti-Money Laundering Division (AMLD). https://www.mjib.gov.tw/EditPage/?PageID=3bf48af4-bfbe-41e3-9137-d908e16eb1cc
Ministry of Justice Investigation Bureau (MJIB) (2017b, October 6; updated 2025, May 2) 授權命令. https://www.mjib.gov.tw/EditPage/?PageID=e834cf2f-15cd-4b3b-91f4-33e2ce0cc886
Ministry of Justice Investigation Bureau (MJIB) (2023) Anti-Money Laundering Annual Report, 2023. https://www.mjib.gov.tw/EditPage/?PageID=46098253-f0e9-46e4-9832-b96e17e00c71. https://www.mjib.gov.tw/userfiles/files/35-%E6%B4%97%E9%8C%A2%E9%98%B2%E5%88%B6%E8%99%95/files/%E6%B4%97%E9%8C%A2%E9%98%B2%E5%88%B6%E8%99%95-EN/2023yearbook.pdf
Silva PG (2019) Recent developments in EU legislation on anti-money laundering and terrorist financing. New J Eur Crim Law 10(1):57–67. https://doi.org/10.1177/2032284419840442
Sunrise Attorney-at-Law (2024) 【刑事】刑事訴訟法修法三讀通過 科技偵查法源授權(一). https://sunrisetaipei.com/20240806-2/. Accessed 2 Dec 2024

Wang WY, Chiu YLA (2014) The Defining characteristics of the legal family in East Asia. In: Wang WY (ed) Codification in East Asia. Springer, pp 3–18. https://doi.org/10.1007/978-3-319-03446-1_1

Chapter 6
Conclusion

Abstract This chapter in conclusion summarizes key insights to help navigate a global financial order that is more inclusive and sustainable.

In conclusion, the year 2024 will be remembered as a pivotal moment in the universal fight against ML and TF. In the western hemisphere, the EU fulfilled its pledge to put into practice a comprehensive AML/CFT package after three years of legislative review. Composed of three regulations and a directive, the reforms roll out a new supranational authority with expert skills and concentrated powers. Headquartered in Frankfurt am Main, Germany, AMLA's seat is in the immediate vicinity of the ECB, the ESRB and EIOPA, with the ESMA and EBA not far away in the neighbouring country of France. Retaining a trajectory of supervisory convergence, AMLA transcends the European System of Financial Supervision (ESFS) and the Single Supervisory Mechanism (SSM), as it ventures into new terrain by assuming both micro- and macro-prudential oversight over financial and non-financial entities. The integrated framework benefits from synergies that flow from linking human and technical resources, while being counterbalanced by the principles of autonomous decisionmaking and decentralization. Internally serving as a coordinator and mediator between Member States, AMLA is also endowed with external mandates and as such will be a vital partner for transnational collaboration. Like never before, there will be unchartered gateways to reach out and for stakeholders abroad (e.g. official authorities, expert advisers, "any person whose opinion may be of interest") to provide their input.[1]

The institutional restructuring is accompanied by a harmonized rulebook that sends a message to outsiders, exhorting them to comply with tougher prescriptions. Gatekeepers of the EU financial system—notably service providers the fields of crypto-assets, crowdfunding, investment migration and sports—are subject to minimum registration requirements and obliged to conduct customer due diligence. Anonymous products and relations (including large cash transactions) are outlawed, and customers from all backgrounds (along with personal ties and associations,

[1] AMLA Regulation, Art. 62 ("Meetings of the General Board"). See Chap. 3, Table 3.7.

Y. L. A. Chiu, *Money Laundering and Terrorist Financing*,
SpringerBriefs in Law and Regulation & Innovation,
https://doi.org/10.1007/978-981-96-6654-6_6

beneficiaries, and other involved parties) are scrutinized holistically in view of individual profiles and dynamic risk factors, once certain transaction thresholds are surpassed. The efficacy in doing so can be optimized by recruiting remote partners via outsourcing and third party reliance.

Especially zooming in on BOs, refined techniques are prescribed to unveil their true identity. Above all, nominee directors and shareholders, foreign legal entities, express trusts and similar arrangements are compelled to disclose their BOs when entering into business relationships with obliged entities, public procurement contracts, or acquiring real estate or certain high-value goods in the Union. Vigorous cross-checking through various information channels ensures that beneficial ownership registers remain up-to-date. Concomitantly, progressive strategies counter threats originating from third countries, which are rated with regard to the effectiveness of their AML/CTF systems, nor can multinational enterprises in remote corners of the world avoid group-wide supervision. A liberal explanation of the term "third countries" envisioning any jurisdiction or autonomous territory outside the Union maximizes the cogency of the EU regime and is all the more an incentive for outlying jurisdictions such as Taiwan to stay alert.

Severe consquences entailing fines, nonpecuniary administrative measures, criminal sanctions, and even the invalidity of business relationships target a bigger number of persons, thereby underpinning the persuasiveness of sweeping reforms. All this could turn the tides and make it less probable for perpetrators to escape. Seen from this dimension, the EU's groundbreaking policies could have extraterritorrial effects far beyond its borders (Scott 2014) and even serve as a catalyst for third countries to ramp up their AML/CTF standards in conformity with EU norms. As the latter normally reflect a widespread consensus that has been forged within specialized networks such as the FATF, EU proposals simultaneously accelerate the adoption of international recommendations. This way, the repercussions will traverse the European continent and be multiplied around the globe.

As a matter of fact, in the eastern hemisphere, the island nation of Taiwan—officially known as the Republic of China—ratified a bold blueprint to repel fraud in July 2024, just weeks after the new EU legislation was published. Driven by a desire to be in consonance with APG and FATF recommendations, the evolution of domestic laws and regulations bears witness how various codifications and statutes from the EU and its Member States served as paragons, generating a mixed synthesis that is adapted to Taiwan's unique legal and social environment, but also mostly in tune with the EU. Evincing fascinating parallels in terms of historic timelines, underlying motives, employed terminology and modus operandi, an in-depth analysis corroborates how common patterns are not mere coincidences but linked to a preceding impetus.

A striking feature in this context is the pervasive use of administrative regulations that are adopted by competent authorities to complement the MLCA. Arguably, the inclination to defer to the executive branch might be partly rooted in a habit of flexible, non-confrontational administrative guidance implanted in Asian civilizations. The rise of avant-garde service providers for virtual assets and third-party payments from the regulatory level to the rank of fully-fledged obliged entities at the legislative level, exemplifies how this tradition has fostered pilot projects, allowing startups to harness their inventions, while shielding consumers against excessive risks. Undisputedly, this legislative technique of devolution, which is also a distinctive trait of the EU architecture, is a useful tool to keep pace with rapid changes. A drawback of such a discretionary, informal approach is that it conforms to a lesser extent with doctrines of democratic legitimization and legal clarity, making it harder to foretell with certainty the future ramifications. All the more, the coming years will be a crucial test period to stay the course and enable smooth operations of recent reforms.

With huge adversities lying ahead, the mission of the EU and its partners is clear: They must switch from a passive attitude of procrastination to proactive empowerment, cope with a reality that connects with cyberspace (Mooij 2024; Wang et al. 2021) and magnify their international clout. As time is of the essence and the only constant is change, it is paramount to embrace challenges, thereby transforming them into opportunities. This includes the deployment of cutting-edge technology to detect ML (Pavlidis 2023), without replacing seasoned officers entrusted to carry out delicate tasks that require an unwavering sense of devotion and discernment (Chan et al. 2020).

Surely, all governments—including smaller jurisdictions like Taiwan—constitute an undeniable part of a common chain. Even the most robust system will in the end only be as strong as its weakest link (European Commission 2020, p. 9; Schlarb 2022, p. 75). The magic solution that will fix dangerous flaws and make the global financial system resistant against criminal attacks is inclusiveness. Since national and regional solutions will unfold their full potency to the extent that they are delivered in concert with the international community, stakeholders at all levels, horizontal as well as vertical, are thus encouraged to engage with each other in constructive ways. In a setting that is permeated by equity and dignity for all (Saul 2024), it will be feasible to build a secure financial system that is more sustainable and resilient. In this sense, the author hopes that this book contributes to building bridges between the east and the west, to celebrate common achievements, while deepening a mutual understanding of unique legal cultures.

References

Chan T-E, Chan Y-H, Lin S-P (2020) A causal model of the declaration intention of banks for suspected money-laundering transactions based on organizational commitment perspective. J Money Laundering Control 23(2):403–425. https://doi.org/10.1108/JMLC-12-2019-0098

European Commission (2020, May 7) Action Plan for a comprehensive Union policy on preventing money laundering and terrorist financing. https://eur-lex.europa.eu/legal-content/EN/TXT/?uri=PI_COM:C(2020)2800

Mooij A (2024) Regulating the Metaverse economy: how to prevent money laundering and the financing of terrorism. Springer, Cham. https://doi.org/10.1007/978-3-031-46417-1Cham.

Pavlidis G (2023) Deploying artificial intelligence for anti-money laundering and asset recovery: the dawn of a new era. J Money Laundering Control 26(7):155–166. https://doi.org/10.1108/JMLC-03-2023-0050

Saul B (2024) Vision and priorities. Report of the Special Rapporteur on the promotion and protection of human rights and fundamental freedoms while countering terrorism. https://documents.un.org/doc/undoc/gen/g24/000/66/pdf/g2400066.pdf
Schlarb DD (2022) Rethinking anti-money laundering supervision: the Single Supervisory Mechanism - a model for a European anti-money laundering supervisor? New J EurCrim Law 13(1):69–90. https://doi.org/10.1177/20322844221085949
Scott J (2014) Extraterritoriality and territorial extension in EU law. Am J Comp Law 62(1):87–126. https://doi.org/10.5131/AJCL.2013.0009
Wang S-YK, Hsieh M-L, Chang CK-M, Jiang P-S, Dallier DJ (2021) Collaboration between law enforcement agencies in combating cybercrime: implications of a Taiwanese case study about ATM hacking. Int J Offender Ther Comp Criminol 65(4):390–408. https://doi.org/10.1177/0306624X20952391

Appendix

Relevant laws and regulations mentioned in this book are listed below in chronological order.

Primary EU Legislation[1]

Consolidated versions of the Treaty on European Union and the Treaty on the Functioning of the European Union, OJ C 202, 7.6.2016, p. 1–388.

Secondary EU Legislation (Directives and Regulations)[2]

Council Directive 91/308/EEC of 10 June 1991 on prevention of the use of the financial system for the purpose of money laundering, OJ L 166, 28.6.1991, p. 77–82 (1st AMLD).

Directive 2001/97/EC of the European Parliament and of the Council of 4 December 2001 amending Council Directive 91/308/EEC on prevention of the use of the financial system for the purpose of money laundering, OJ L 344, 28.12.2001, p. 76–82 (2nd AMLD).

Directive 2005/60/EC of the European Parliament and of the Council of 26 October 2005 on the prevention of the use of the financial system for the purpose of money laundering and terrorist financing, OJ L 309, 25.11.2005, p. 15–36 (3rd AMLD).

[1] Available at the official website of the European Union at https://eur-lex.europa.eu/.

[2] Available at the official website of the European Union at https://eur-lex.europa.eu/.

Y. L. A. Chiu, *Money Laundering and Terrorist Financing*, SpringerBriefs in Law and Regulation & Innovation,
https://doi.org/10.1007/978-981-96-6654-6

Directive 2009/110/EC of the European Parliament and of the Council of 16 September 2009 on the taking up, pursuit and prudential supervision of the business of electronic money institutions, OJ L 267, 10.10.2009, p. 7–17.

Regulation (EU) No 1092/2010 of the European Parliament and of the Council of 24 November 2010 on European Union macro-prudential oversight of the financial system and establishing a European Systemic Risk Board OJ L 331, 15.12.2010, p. 1–11 (ESRB Regulation).

Regulation (EU) No. 1093/2010 of the European Parliament and of the Council of 24 November 2010 establishing a European Supervisory Authority (European Banking Authority), OJ L 331, 15.12.2010, p. 12–47 (EBA Regulation).

Regulation (EU) No 1094/2010 of the European Parliament and of the Council of 24 November 2010 establishing a European Supervisory Authority (European Insurance and Occupational Pensions Authority), OJ L 331, 15.12.2010, p. 48–83 (EIOPA Regulation).

Regulation (EU) No 1095/2010 of the European Parliament and of the Council of 24 November 2010 establishing a European Supervisory Authority (European Securities and Markets Authority), OJ L 331, 15.12.2010, p. 84–119 (ESMA Regulation).

Directive 2013/34/EU of the European Parliament and of the Council of 26 June 2013 on the annual financial statements, consolidated financial statements and related reports of certain types of undertakings, OJ L 182, 29.6.2013, p. 19–76.

Directive 2013/36/EU of the European Parliament and of the Council of 26 June 2013 on access to the activity of credit institutions and the prudential supervision of credit institutions and investment firms, OJ L 176, 27.6.2013, p. 338–436 (Capital Requirements Directive).

Council Regulation (EU) No. 1024/2013 of 15 October 2013 conferring specific tasks on the European Central Bank concerning policies relating to the prudential supervision of credit institutions, OJ L 287, 29.10.2013, p. 63–89 (Basic SSM Regulation).

Directive 2014/42/EU of the European Parliament and of the Council of 3 April 2014 on the freezing and confiscation of instrumentalities and proceeds of crime in the European Union, OJ L 127, 29.4.2014, p. 39–50.

Regulation (EU) No. 468/2014 of the European Central Bank of 16 April 2014 establishing the framework for cooperation within the Single Supervisory Mechanism between the European Central Bank and national competent authorities and with national designated authorities (ECB/SSM Framework Regulation), OJ L 141, 14.5.2014, p. 1–50.

Directive (EU) 2015/849 of the European Parliament and of the Council of 20 May 2015 on the prevention of the use of the financial system for the purposes of money laundering or terrorist financing, OJ L 141, 5.6.2015, p. 73–117 (4th AMLD).

Directive (EU) 2015/2366 of the European Parliament and of the Council of 25 November 2015 on payment services in the internal market, OJ L 337, 23.12.2015, p. 35–127.

Directive (EU) 2017/541 of the European Parliament and of the Council of 15 March 2017 on combating terrorism and replacing Council Framework Decision

2002/475/JHA and amending Council Decision 2005/671/JHA, OJ L 88, 31.3.2017, p. 6–21.

Directive (EU) 2017/1132 of the European Parliament and of the Council of 14 June 2017 relating to certain aspects of company law, OJ L 169, 30/06/2017, p. 46–127.

Directive (EU) 2018/843 of the European Parliament and of the Council of 30 May 2018 amending Directive (EU) 2015/849 on the prevention of the use of the financial system for the purposes of money laundering or terrorist financing, OJ L 156, 19.6.2018, p. 43–74 (5th AMLD).

Directive (EU) 2018/1673 of the European Parliament and of the Council of 23 October 2018 on combating money laundering by criminal law, OJ L 284, 12.11.2018, p. 22–30.

Commission Delegated Regulation (EU) 2019/758 of 31 January 2019 supplementing Directive (EU) 2015/849 of the European Parliament and of the Council with regard to regulatory technical standards for the minimum action and the type of additional measures credit and financial institutions must take to mitigate money laundering and terrorist financing risk in certain third countries, OJ L 125, 14.5.2019, p. 4–10.

Directive (EU) 2019/1937 of the European Parliament and of the Council of 23 October 2019 on the protection of persons who report breaches of Union law, OJ L 305, 26.11.2019, p. 17–56 (Whistleblower Protection Directive).

Directive (EU) 2019/2177 of the European Parliament and of the Council of 18 December 2019 amending Directive 2009/138/EC on the taking-up and pursuit of the business of Insurance and Reinsurance (Solvency II), Directive 2014/65/EU on markets in financial instruments and Directive (EU) 2015/849 on the prevention of the use of the financial system for the purposes of money-laundering or terrorist financing, OJ L 334, 27.12.2019, p. 155–163.

Regulation (EU) 2020/1503 of the European Parliament and of the Council of 7 October 2020 on European crowdfunding service providers for business, OJ L 347, 20.10.2020, p. 1–49 (ECSP Regulation).

Regulation (EU) 2023/1113 of the European Parliament and of the Council of 31 May 2023 on information accompanying transfers of funds and certain crypto-assets and amending Directive (EU) 2015/849, OJ L 150, 9.6.2023, p. 1–39, ELI: http://data.europa.eu/eli/reg/2023/1113/oj (TFR).

Regulation (EU) 2023/1114 of the European Parliament and of the Council of 31 May 2023 on markets in crypto-assets, OJ L 150, 9.6.2023, p. 40–205 (MiCA Regulation).

Regulation (EU) 2024/1620 of the European Parliament and of the Council of 31 May 2024 establishing the Authority for Anti-Money Laundering and Countering the Financing of Terrorism and amending Regulations (EU) No. 1093/2010, (EU) No. 1094/2010 and (EU) No. 1095/2010, OJ L, 2024/1620, 19.6.2024, ELI: http://data.europa.eu/eli/reg/2024/1620/oj (AMLA Regulation).

Regulation (EU) 2024/1624 of the European Parliament and of the Council of 31 May 2024 on the prevention of the use of the financial system for the purposes of money laundering or terrorist financing, OJ L, 2024/1624, 19.6.2024, ELI: http://data.europa.eu/eli/reg/2024/1624/oj (AML/CFT Regulation).

Directive (EU) 2024/1640 of the European Parliament and of the Council of 31 May 2024 on the mechanisms to be put in place by Member States for the prevention of the use of the financial system for the purposes of money laundering or terrorist financing, amending Directive (EU) 2019/1937, and amending and repealing Directive (EU) 2015/849, OJ L, 2024/1640, 19.6.2024, ELI: http://data.europa.eu/eli/dir/2024/1640/oj (6th AMLD).

Other European Laws

Germany
Criminal Code[3]
1998, amended 2021

United Kingdom
The Money Laundering, Terrorist Financing and Transfer of Funds (Information on the Payer) Regulations 2017[4]
2017

Codes and Statutory Laws in the Republic of China (Taiwan)[5]

Code of Criminal Procedure
刑事訴訟法
1928, amended 2024

Company Act
公司法
1929, amended 2021

Criminal Code of the Republic of China
中華民國刑法
1935, amended 2024

[3] Available at the webpage of the German Federal Ministry of Justice at https://www.gesetze-im-internet.de/englisch_stgb/englisch_stgb.html#p2435 and https://www.bgbl.de/xaver/bgbl/start.xav#__bgbl__%2F%2F*%5B%40attr_id%3D%27bgbl121s0327.pdf%27%5D__1723778687010.

[4] Available at The National Archives of the UK government at https://www.legislation.gov.uk/uksi/2017/692/contents/made.

[5] Available at the Laws & Regulations Database of the Republic of China (Taiwan) at https://law.moj.gov.tw/Eng/.

Water Pollution Control Act
水污染防治法
1974, amended 2018

Air Pollution Control Act
空氣污染防制法
1975, amended 2018

Act Governing Food Safety and Sanitation
食品安全衛生管理法
1975, amended 2019

Money Laundering Control Act (MLCA)
洗錢防制法
1996, amended 2024

The Communication Security and Surveillance Act
通訊保障及監察法
1999, amended 2024

Counter-Terrorism Financing Act
資恐防制法
2016, amended 2018

Fraud Crime Hazard Prevention Act
詐欺犯罪危害防制條例
2024

Administrative Regulations in the Republic of China (Taiwan)[6]

MOEA
Regulations Governing AML/CFT for Jewelry Businesses
銀樓業防制洗錢與打擊資恐辦法
2011, amended 2021

FSC
The Act Governing Electronic Payment Institutions
電子支付機構管理條例
2015, amended 2023

Ministry of Justice
PEPs Standards

---

[6] Available at the Laws & Regulations Database of the Republic of China (Taiwan) at https://law.moj.gov.tw/Eng/.

Standards for Determining the Scope of Politically Exposed Persons Entrusted with Prominent Public Function, Their Family Members and Close Associates
重要政治性職務之人與其家庭成員及有密切關係之人範圍認定標準
2017, amended 2024

Council of Agriculture
Agricultural FIs Regulations
Regulations Governing AML of Agricultural FIs
農業金融機構防制洗錢辦法.
2017, amended 2018

FSC
Accountants Regulations
Regulations Governing AML/CFT for Certified Public Accountants
會計師防制洗錢及打擊資恐辦法
2017, amended 2020

Ministry of Justice
Attorneys Regulations
Regulations on Anti-Money Laundering & Countering the Financing of Terrorism Operations Matters Conducted by Attorneys
律師辦理防制洗錢及打擊資恐作業辦法
2017, amended 2024

Ministry of Interior
Brokerages Regulations
Regulations Governing AML/CTF for Land Administration Agents and Real Estate Brokerages
地政士及不動產經紀業防制洗錢及打擊資恐辦法
2017, amended 2021

FSC
FIs Regulations
Regulations Governing AML of FIs
金融機構防制洗錢辦法
2017, amended 2021

FSC
Experimentation Act
Financial Technology Development and Innovative Experimentation Act
金融科技發展與創新實驗條例
2018

FSC
Leasing Enterprises Regulations
Regulations Governing AML of Financial Leasing Enterprises
辦理融資性租賃業務事業防制洗錢辦法
2018

FSC
Regulations Governing Internal Audit and Internal Control System of AML/CFT of Banking Business and Other FIs Designated by the FSC
銀行業及其他經金融監督管理委員會指定之金融機構防制洗錢及打擊資恐內部控制與稽核制度實施辦法
2018, amended 2021

Council of Agriculture
Regulations Governing Internal Audit and Internal Control System of AML/CT of Agricultural FIs
防制洗錢與打擊資恐內部控制及稽核制度實施辦法
2018

MOEA
Regulations Governing Reporting and Management of Information on Article 22 Bis of the Company Act
公司法第二十二條之一資料申報及管理辦法
2018

Judicial Yuan
Notaries Regulations
Regulations Governing AML/CTF for Notaries
公證人防制洗錢及打擊資恐辦法
2018, amended 2024

FSC
Experimentation Regulations
Regulations Governing AML/CTF of Financial Technology Innovative Experimentation
金融科技創新實驗防制洗錢及打擊資恐辦法
2019

Ministry of Justice
Regulations on Competent Authorities Governing Specific Foundations for AML/CTF
主管機關辦理特定財團法人洗錢及資恐防制辦法
2019

Executive Yuan
Decree no. 1100167722
2021, April 7

FSC
VC Regulations
Regulations Governing AML/CFT for Enterprises Handling VC Platform or Transaction
虛擬通貨平台及交易業務事業防制洗錢及打擊資恐辦法
2021, amended 2024 and renamed

VA Regulations
Regulations Governing AML/CFT for Enterprises or Persons Providing Virtual Asset Services
提供虛擬資產服務之事業或人員防制洗錢及打擊資恐辦法
2021, amended 2024

Executive Yuan
Decree no. 1100181600
2021, Aug. 18

Ministry of Digital Affairs
Third-Party Payment Regulations
Regulations Governing AML/CFT for Enterprises or Persons Providing Third-Party Payment Services
提供第三方支付服務之事業或人員防制洗錢及打擊資恐辦法
2022, amended 2024

Ministry of Justice
Measures for Non-trust Sectors
Measures for Filing, Updating and Reporting of Trustee Information and Disclosure of Trust Status for Non-trust Sectors under Article 11, Paragraph 6 of the Money Laundering Control Act
洗錢防制法第十一條第六項非信託業之受託人資訊申報更新申報及信託地位揭露辦法
2024, Nov. 25

FSC
VASP Registration Regulations
Regulations Governing AML Registration of Enterprises or Persons Providing Virtual Asset Services
提供虛擬資產服務之事業或人員洗錢防制登記辦法
2024, Nov. 26

The manufacturer's authorised representative in the EU is Springer Nature Customer Service Centre GmbH, Europaplatz 3, 69115 Heidelberg, Germany. If you have any concerns regarding our products, please contact ProductSafety@springernature.com

Printed and bound by CPI Group (UK) Ltd, Croydon, CR0 4YY
01/10/2026
02225880-0010